Dragonflies:
Q&A GUIDE

Dragonflies:
Q&A GUIDE

Fascinating Facts About Their Life in the Wild

Ann Cooper

STACKPOLE
BOOKS

Published by
STACKPOLE BOOKS
5067 Ritter Road
Mechanicsburg, PA 17055
www.stackpolebooks.com

Printed in China

10 9 8 7 6 5 4 3 2 1

FIRST EDITION

Cover design by Tessa Sweigert
Cover photos by Rob Hainer/Shutterstock.com and CreativeNature.nl/Shutterstock.com

Photos by the author except where noted.

Library of Congress Cataloging-in-Publication Data

Cooper, Ann (Ann C.)
  Dragonflies Q&A guide : fascinating facts about their life in the wild /
Ann Cooper. — First edition.
      pages cm
  ISBN 978-0-8117-1326-9 (pbk.)
  1. Dragonflies—Miscellanea. I. Title. II. Title: Dragonflies.
  QL520.C65 2014
  595.7'33—dc23
                              2014003216

Contents

What are a dragonfly's legs like?
Why do many dragonflies have hairy legs?
Can dragonflies climb up windows as flies do?
How many legs do dragonfly larvae have?
How do dragonflies breathe?
Do dragonflies have blood?
Does a dragonfly have a heart?
Do dragonflies pee and poop?
What kind of brains do dragonflies have, and can they learn?
Do adult dragonfly males and females look the same?
Why can dragonflies of the same species vary in size as adults?
Do adult dragonflies change their appearance as they age?
What makes a dragonfly's color?
Do dragonflies keep their color after they die?
Why do structural colors fade?
What are a dragonfly's wings made of?
How strong are dragonfly wings?
How do dragonflies fly?
How fast do dragonfly wings beat?
Can dragonflies fly backwards?
How fast can dragonflies fly?
What happens if a dragonfly's wings are damaged?

What is the largest dragonfly in the world?
What is the smallest dragonfly in the world?
What is the largest dragonfly in the United States?
What is the smallest dragonfly in North America?
How much does a dragonfly weigh?

Do dragonflies live everywhere?
What kind of watery habitats do dragonflies inhabit?
What makes a good dragonfly habitat?
What is meant by the terms fliers and perchers?
Are all dragonflies predators?
How do dragonflies catch their food?
Do dragonflies eat as they fly?
With which predators do dragonflies compete for food?
What predators eat dragonflies?
Are red dragonflies poisonous to predators?

Do dragonfly wing patches deflect predators, as butterfly
    "eyespots" do?
Why do dragonflies hunt near traffic lights?
What dangers do dragonflies face?
How do dragonflies defend themselves?
When are dragonflies most active?
Are dragonflies active at night?
Where do dragonflies sleep?
How do dragonflies stay safe when they're roosting?
How do dragonflies stay warm?
How do dragonflies stay warm in areas of cold winters?
How does a dragonfly keep from baking in the sun?
Do dragonflies drink?
Do dragonflies come to flowers?
Do dragonflies groom themselves?
What are dragonflies doing when you see them far from water?
Why do dragonflies swarm?
Can adult dragonflies still swim?
What are dragonflies doing when they go out and back from a
    perch by the pond?
What are dragonflies doing when two together fly over the pond?
How long can dragonflies stay underwater?
How long do dragonflies live?
Was that dragonfly buzzing near my head really following me?

How do dragonflies grow (what is their life cycle)?
What are odonate eggs like?
Where and how do dragonflies lay their eggs?
How do dragonflies know where to lay their eggs?
How long does a dragonfly stay as an egg?
Why do dragonflies lay so many eggs?
Are the seed-like blobs seen on some damsel- and dragonflies
    misplaced eggs?
What are dragonfly larvae like?
How long does a dragonfly stay as a larva?
What are exuviae?
How do dragonflies "know" when to emerge?
What is meant by the rendezvous?
How do dragonfly males and females get together?
What is the mating wheel?

Introduction

Several years ago, I attended a class on dragonflies and damselflies given by my local nature association. The two-day class—an eye-opener—radically changed my wild focus. How could I, a naturalist and nature writer, have spent so many hours of my life in the outdoors and not have noticed the scores of species and the wondrous variety of forms, colors, and behaviors of these stunning insects? Shame on me!

Although Colorado is hardly an epicenter of dragonfly and damselfly activity, from late April to the end of October each year I am obsessed with these creatures. To learn as much as I am able to about why they look and act the way they do, I'd need several more lifetimes.

The study of dragonflies and damselflies—or "odonates" as they're sometimes called—is easier for hobby watchers now than it was in the past. Even if we can't sneak up on our quarry as easily as we'd like, close-focus binoculars and digital cameras are a huge asset. There are also many excellent field guides to help identify dragonflies and damselflies. Most of the books are user-friendly and rely on superb photographs and illustrations to guide the reader to the most probable answer. So far, I haven't found an equivalent compact, easy-to-read, fast-fact source that satisfies my avid curiosity about the rest of the story and helps me answer unexpected questions that crop up when I am teaching on the trail. How do odonates eat, sleep, mate, and survive the winter? What's the gossip about "odes": their origins, their naming, and their reputation in various cultures? There's so much that is fascinating about these creatures, beyond just what species they happen to be.

What follows is a collection of questions I've asked and questions that others have asked me. I know the list is incomplete—the questions keep coming—but it's a start.

How does this book work?

This book can be read straight through or dipped into, as the mood takes you. A list of questions follows. These are posed in different ways, since there's no way to guess how an individual reader will ask the question to which he or she seeks an answer. There's also some overlap in answers. In some places, links lead you to similar topics that address the question from a slightly different angle. Words in bold appear in the glossary (see page 96). They occur in bold only at their first occurrence in the book. If you are a "dipper" and come across an unfamiliar word in plain text, try the glossary first.

What's in a Name?

What is a dragonfly?

In many books, the name "dragonfly" is used as shorthand for both dragonflies and damselflies. I'll use "dragonfly" or "odonate" when I mean both dragonflies *and* damselflies and when the information applies to both. If information applies only to damselflies, I will specifically say so.

Dragonflies are insects. As adults, they have all the body parts you'd expect to find in a typical adult insect: head, thorax, abdomen, legs, wings, eyes, antennae, and mouthparts.

The head is large and appears to be mostly eyes. A dragonfly can turn its head this way and that with lightning-fast movements. It has wraparound compound eyes that give it an almost 360-degree view of prey or approaching predators. In addition, it has three small simple eyes, or **ocelli**, that are sensitive to changes in light intensity. It has a pair of bristle-like antennae on the upper front of its head. These are usually tiny in comparison to those of butterflies or moths, and are much less obvious.

The thorax, or the middle section of the body, is the point of attachment of three pairs of legs and two pairs of wings. The legs are jointed and usually spiny. The last segment, called the **tarsus**, is hook-tipped so the dragonfly can cling to perches. The wings are gauzy and fragile looking, although they are surprisingly tough and sturdy once they harden after hatching. The four wings are able to work independently of one another, enabling the insect to be stunningly agile in the air. Dragonflies

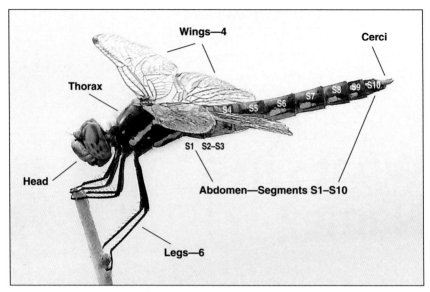

Body parts of a typical dragonfly show it to be an insect.

can zoom out and back, rise and fall, hover, turn on a dime, land at high speed, and even fly backwards for short distances.

The abdomen, the third body part, is long and relatively skinny. Claspers, or **cerci**, are part of the mating apparatus and are located at the tip of the abdomen.

How do dragonflies get their names?

A formal scientific name is given to a dragonfly when it is first described as a new species in scientific literature. The name consists of two parts, genus and species, according to the standard (Linnaean) system of classification. These names are Latin (or Latinized) or Greek and may describe the dragonfly, identify where it's from, or honor a scientist involved in its discovery or identification. These names are universal, ensuring that there is no ambiguity or confusion when discussing a particular species anywhere in the world.

Common names are not universal. Originally, vernacular names grew as part of everyday language. Even the name "dragonfly" suggests that people in the English-speaking world at least regarded these insects with some dread. Dragonflies have also been called Horse Stingers, Devil's Darning Needles, Hobgoblin Flies, and Snake Killers, to mention just a few. It's telling that these names reflected what people thought the insects did (see page 83). Yikes!

The male Blue-eyed Darner has vivid blue eyes.

In North America, common names have been standardized by the Dragonfly Society of the Americas. (See the Resources section on page 98.) Many of the names are evocative, make good sense, and are easy to remember. For example, the Blue-eyed Darner (*Rhionaeschna multicolor*) has incredibly blue eyes. The Autumn Meadowhawk is likely to be seen in fall. The Dot-tailed Whiteface does have a white face, and the male has a prominent white dot on the upper surface of his abdomen. The Vesper Bluet is commonly seen from late afternoon until dusk.

Common names may also come in handy if you are sharing information with people uncomfortable with using scientific names. However, if you get seriously hooked on this group of insects, you may want to become familiar with the scientific names to make the most of this passion.

Elsewhere in the world, common names may be agreed upon within a specific country but can differ from other countries speaking the same language. For example, I've looked for odonates, or "odes," in both North America and the United Kingdom and have had to remember that darners and meadowhawks (North America) are hawkers and darters (United Kingdom). This is another good reason to learn some Latin, if you wish to avoid this language barrier and the misunderstandings that may follow.

Where do dragonflies belong in the animal kingdom?

Scientists sort all living things into categories of similar creatures, like with like, to handle the copious information and relationships between them. These categories start out broad and get ever more exclusive. (If you like, this system is not much different than sorting your clothing shirts with shirts and socks with socks, then further sorting shirts by sleeve length and socks by color.)

The Common Green Darner fits into the hierarchy like this:

Kingdom Animalia—Animals
  Phylum Arthropoda—Arthropods ("jointed legs")
    Class Insecta—Insects
      Order Odonata—Dragonflies and Damselflies ("toothed ones")
        Suborder Anisoptera—Dragonflies
          Family Aeshnidae—Darners
            Genus *Anax*
              Species *junius*—Common Green Darner

In referring to this species, you'd use the binomial of genus and species: *Anax junius*, Common Green Darner.

Are dragonfly scientific names set in stone?

No scientific names are set in stone. Over the years, some species that scientists thought were new later turned out to be previously described specimens, perhaps of a different sex or from a different locality. In that case, the newer name is rejected in favor of the original scientific name. In other cases, species that scientists considered distinct turned out to be similar enough to lump together as a subspecies of an existing species. For example, the small dragonfly once known as the Western Meadowhawk in Colorado, *Sympetrum occidentale*, was reassigned and became a subspecies of the Band-winged Meadowhawk, *Sympetrum semicinctum*. Depending on which book you consult, you might come across either one of these names.

As scientists learn more about the relationships between different groups of animals, they may realize that a species previously thought to belong in one group is more closely related to a different group. In this case, the species may be reassigned to a different genus and its name may change. DNA analysis is a major tool in establishing or reassigning relationships between groups of animals. As more DNA analysis takes place, there will probably be name adjustments.

Above: A Band-winged Meadowhawk male, once known as the Western Meadowhawk in Colorado.
On previous page: A Common Green Darner (Anax junius) *is easy to overlook when roosting.*

A centipede has one pair of legs on each body segment.

What animals are a dragonfly's closest relatives?

A dragonfly's closest relatives are other insects, with mayflies thought to be the most similar. Insects share features with other **arthropods**, or animals with jointed legs. The phylum Arthropoda includes millipedes, centipedes, crustaceans, ticks, and spiders.

All arthropods are alike in five basic ways:

- They show left/right symmetry. That means the left side is a mirror image of the right side, and they have a definite head and tail end.
- They have segmented bodies. You can see this in the photo of the centipede.
- They have numerous paired limbs. A centipede has one pair of legs on each body segment. The number may not be precisely a hundred, but it is large. A millipede has two pairs of legs on each body segment, probably not a thousand, but possibly several hundreds.
- The legs are jointed for ease of movement.
- Above all, these animals have **exoskeletons**, or hard shells on the outside.

These five features influence the animals' growth patterns, behaviors, and lives.

What is an exoskeleton?

An exoskeleton is a hard shell located on the outside of the body. It performs the same support function for arthropods that a bony, internal skeleton does for us.

The exoskeleton is formed from a horny substance called **chitin**, a tough, nitrogen-containing polysaccharide. This armor-like chitin protects the insect's body and prevents the insect from drying out.

Like a medieval knight's armor, an exoskeleton allows movement. Joints must be able to bend, so the shell between the different sections of leg (the femur, tibia, and tarsus) is less hefty and more pliable than the material covering the leg segments themselves. In the same way, the adjoining segments of the abdomen are not rigidly encased in chitin so that the whole abdomen can wiggle and curve significantly in some planes.

What's the downside to having an exoskeleton?

The biggest downside to having an exoskeleton is that it must be relatively rigid to be an effective support. Because an exoskeleton can't stretch, the only way an animal with an exoskeleton can grow is to crack out of one shell when it becomes too tight and expand like crazy before the new exoskeletal layer has time to harden.

The process of shedding the exoskeleton is called molting, and it is a very vulnerable time for any arthropod. At that time, the soft-shelled animal makes easy pickings for a lucky predator. In the case of dragonflies, most of the molts take place in the water as that is where the **larva** (sometimes called a **nymph**, or **naiad**) usually lives as it grows from a newly hatched egg to a near-adult. The last molt takes place when the larval insect crawls out of the watery habitat in which it has been living, loses its last larval shell, and emerges as an adult. Adult dragonflies do not molt again. They have reached their full size and the last part of their life cycle.

Cast-off exoskeleton of a dragonfly.

What are the other constraints imposed by an exoskeleton?

An exoskeleton limits the size to which an arthropod can grow. (Aren't you glad that bear-sized bugs are impossible?) There are several possible reasons for this.

When an arthropod sheds its shell, the soft body inside has little means of support. It sags under gravity like a water-filled balloon. This doesn't matter for small bodies because they can hold themselves in shape by ingesting air. In doing so, they increase the pressure exerted by their **hemolymph** (insect blood) until the soft **cuticle** becomes hardened again. But would a larger, heavier body deform much more and become more blob-like? Would the new shell harden around the now-splayed soft body? The mind boggles!

The weight of an exoskeleton even on a tiny insect is not trivial. If the insect were to double in size, the body volume and weight would be cubed. For every enlargement, the exoskeleton is heavier and the animal needs stronger legs and stronger muscles to move the larger body. Beyond a certain point, you could imagine the legs would splay under the weight of the huge body. Insects' muscles are internal and exert force on the inside of the shells. There's a limit to how big they can grow, unlike mammal muscles which act by exerting force from the outside on interior bones. Mammals can bulk up with almost no limit.

Insects don't have lungs and oxygen-circulating blood. They breathe through tiny holes, called **spiracles**, in their outer shells. The spiracles lead to a system of **trachea** and **tracheoles** (see page 26). Oxygen in the air diffuses through these tracheoles to reach the inner tissues of the body—but not very fast. One theory suggests that if the insect were to grow much larger, the oxygen might not be able to reach the interior cells as effectively, so the metabolism of those cells might not function as it should.

Are dragonflies flies?

Although the word "fly" forms part of their common name, dragonflies are *not* flies. True flies are insects in the order Diptera, or "two-winged." The two wings of the name are the front wings, which are used for flying. The hindwings are tiny knobs called halteres that function as balance organs. In contrast, dragonflies have four full-size wings used for flying.

How many different kinds of dragonflies are there?

This question is almost impossible to answer. First, new species are still being described, so any formal list is subject to change. Second, taxonomists (scientists who specialize in the systematic classification of living things) don't always agree on classification. Some are "lumpers" who combine kinds of odonates into fewer but broader families, genera, and species. Others are "splitters" who split kinds into narrower families, genera, or species.

Roughly, there are more than twenty-five different families of dragonflies, including ten or so dragonfly (Anisoptera) families and around eighteen damselfly (Zygoptera) families. Within these families are

*Above: One of the many Pond Damsels—Plains Forktail (*Ischnura damula*).*
*On previous page: A true fly (*Diptera*) has one pair of wings for flying.*

somewhere between five and six thousand species, depending on how the species are lumped or split.

The largest family seems to be that of the Pond Damsels (Coenagrionidae), with more than 1,100 species. No wonder this is such a challenging group for beginning enthusiasts to identify!

How many kinds of dragonflies and damselflies are there in North America?

Numbers like this can only be accurate at the time of writing. According to the 2012 edition of *The Checklist of North American Odonata*, by Dennis R. Paulson and Sidney W. Dunkle, 462 species of dragonflies and damselflies occur in North America north of Mexico. This could change at any time if species expand their range. Among this number are 326 dragons and 136 damsels.

Which US state has the most kinds of dragonflies?

The center of dragonfly diversity lies in the tropics, so it is no surprise that our warmer and wetter states have an advantage when it comes to species numbers. Texas, being as large as it is, has more dragonflies and damselflies that any other state. The dragonfly-watchers there also keep documenting new species that stray north across the border from Mexico.

If you want to see how your state stacks up, look it up on Odonata Central. The records on this database are increasing by leaps and bounds as more enthusiasts enter their field data for verification. As time goes on, a much clearer picture of the full dragonfly fauna, state by state, will be readily available.

Are there dragonfly fossils?

Of all the animals that live and die, very few become fossils. Certain conditions must be met for fossilization to take place. The animal must die in a suitable place, be overlooked by predators, and fall into the right kind of mud, silt, or other material for preservation. Additionally, the animal must possess enough hard body parts to either leave an impression or have tissues replaced by material that will last. Most important of all the animal must be unearthed again. It's a chancy scenario. Despite all of these conditions, quite a lot of dragonfly fossils have been found.

The oldest fossils date back about 325 million years. They turned up in limestone formations in Germany, and scientists classify them as Protodonata, a now-extinct ancestral group. About 300 million years ago,

WHAT HAPPENED WHEN?

Era	Period	BP=Before Present (in millions of years)	Event
Cenozoic	Quaternary	0–1.7	Humans
	Tertiary	1.7–65	Modern insect genera develop
Mesozoic	Cretaceous	65–135	Flowering plants Insect species multiply
	Jurassic	135–192	First bees and wasps
	Triassic	192–230	First flies
Paleozoic	Permian	230–280	Dragonflies smaller First beetles
	Carboniferous	280–345	Giant dragonflies First recognizable dragonflies
	Devonian	345–405	First insect records

gigantic dragonflies showed up in the fossil record, usually represented by their preserved wings only. Some had a wingspan of up to 720 mm (28 inches)—roughly the same wingspan as a present-day pigeon, or Rock Dove. They became extinct by the end of the Permian era.

About 250 million year ago, fossil dragonfly and damselfly prototypes of much more modest size began to show up. The Solnhofen limestone formations in the German state of Bavaria have been a rich source of these fossils. The area was once a huge inland lagoon and the conditions there seemed ideal for fossil formation. Of course, fossils can't tell details of how the insects lived. These can only be deduced from the body parts that remain in stone—wings, spines on legs, and so on.

Impressions of dragonfly wings have been found in the fossil beds at Florissant, Colorado. They were classified according to careful analysis of the wing veins just as wing veins are used in species identification among living odonates. Some of the largest fossils have been found in limestone formations at Elmo, near Abilene, Kansas. Others have been discovered in Rancho La Brea Tar Pits, natural seeps of tar from underground, in the heart of Los Angeles, California. The rarest fossil odonates, almost all of them damselflies, are those preserved in amber.

Fossil Dragonfly (Libellulium longialatum) *from the Jurassic period, 150 million years BP, found in the Solnhofen limestone formations in Bavaria.*

Why were some ancient dragonflies so huge?

Fossil finds have established that around 300 million years ago there were dragonflies with 28-inch wingspans. One noted ode expert (Philip S. Corbet, author of *Dragonflies: Behavior and Ecology of Odonata*) deduced that the larvae of these giant dragonflies must have been approximately 30 centimeters (almost 12 inches) long. Why the insects were able to grow to that size, given the conventional understanding of the limitations of exoskeletons, is still not completely resolved.

According to the Air Resources Laboratory at NOAA, our air now contains, on average, 20.9476 percent oxygen. Back then, there was about 50 percent more oxygen in the air than there is today. One theory suggests that higher oxygen levels spawned the giant odes. In 2010, biologists reported they had successfully grown dragonflies 15 percent larger than normal by raising them in conditions that mimicked 300 million-year-old oxygen levels on earth. The experimental dragonflies grew faster as well as bigger. The scientists concluded that with more oxygen available to diffuse into body tissues, the insects could grow larger without needing an overwhelmingly large and elaborate tracheal system to deal with their oxygen needs.

Other researchers are skeptical. Higher oxygen levels would also have impacted the larvae if they were water-based then. If the larvae passively absorbed oxygen, what if oxygen were toxic during this time when levels were so high? One way for larvae populations to survive would have been to grow larger. By doing so, body volume would increase faster than body surface area and so the excess oxygen would be effectively diluted.

This is a perfect example of lively scientific debate which may eventually lead to an answer all can accept.

What is a damselfly?

A damselfly is an insect belonging to a suborder within the order Odonata called Zygoptera, which means "same wing." The forewings and hindwings are a similar shape. Anisoptera, dragonflies, have forewings and hindwings of a different shape, the hindwings being wider near the body.

Damselflies are typically frailer, weaker fliers than dragonflies. Many of them, the Pond Damsels especially, glean insects low in the grass and flush when you walk through a meadow. But damselflies usually alight again after flying only a short distance. Many damselflies, especially the bluets, float mere inches above the ground or water surface so easily that they seem to be levitating.

*At right: A damselfly's four wings are of a similar shape: Lyre-tipped Spread-wing (*Lestes unguiculatus*).*
Below: Damselfly dodging around stem.

*A typical dragonfly, Comanche Skimmer (*Libellula comanche*), at rest with its wings out to the side.*

*A typical damselfly, Paiute Dancer (*Argia alberta*), rests with its wings along the abdomen.*

A damselfly's compound eyes are widely separated. At times an individual will "escape" around the back side of a plant stem when you approach and monitor you with one eyelooking around each side of the stalk (see page 13).

What's the difference between dragonflies and damselflies?

The two main subgroups of odonates are Anisoptera (dragonflies) and Zygoptera (damselflies). You can tell them apart using the following rules of thumb.

HOW DO DRAGONFLIES AND DAMSELFLIES COMPARE?	
Dragonflies	**Damselflies**
Large and chunky	Small and dainty
Robust, strong fliers	Frail, weak fliers
Front wings and hindwings are a different shape	Front wings and hindwings are a similar shape
Rest with wings stuck out to the side	Rest with wings folded over the back or loosely angled
Eyes close together or touching at the midline	Eyes well separated, like those of a hammerhead shark
Larva has terminal spines on the abdomen tip	Larva has feathery gills on the abdomen tip

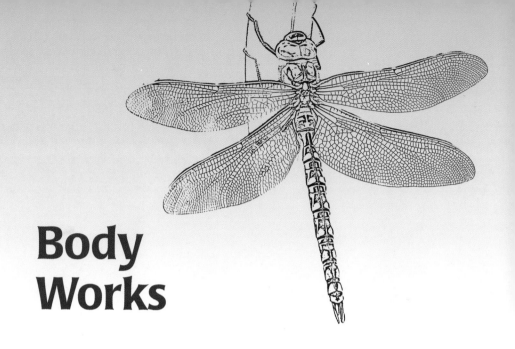

Body
Works

Can dragonflies see well?

Dragonflies can see extremely well. Sight is their primary sense. They have two huge compound eyes, each containing up to 30,000 individual visual units called **ommatidia** (the singular is ommatidium). These visual units fit together in a tight honeycomb pattern. Close-up, you can see that the surface of the compound eye has many, many facets. Some toy stores sell a gadget that supposedly mimics a "bug's eye view," breaking the scene into many discrete dots like an enlarged newspaper image. I have no idea if this correctly represents a dragonfly's view of the world, but for kids and kids-at-heart, it is fun to try.

Regardless of how the visual image appears to the insects, dragonfly eyes are specialized to detect any movement, as you quickly learn when you try and sneak up on these insects. Dragonfly eyes are also capable of discriminating the shape of immobile prey, and they see in color. This is one of the several ways in which dragonflies of the same species recognize that they are two of a kind.

You may also notice a **pseudopupil**, or dark eyespot, on the surface of the compound eye. This is the area of the eye you view head on at a right angle to the alignment of the individual ommatidia. Outside this area the eye appears to be a different color because it reflects light rather than absorbing it. The eyespot is the zone of most acute vision and the part of the eye directed at an object of interest. If there is a blind spot (sometimes you'd wonder), it is the area at a low angle behind the head

*A dragonfly has huge compound eyes, like this Dragonhunter (*Hagenius bre-vistylus*).*

from which you may be able to approach the insect—camera in hand and ever hopeful!

The exact placement of the compound eyes helps you diagnose what type of odonate you are looking at. First, there is a split between dragon-flies (eyes touching at the midline or at least very close together) and damselflies (each compound eye stuck way out on the sides of the head like a hammerhead shark). Second, among the Anisoptera (dragonflies) the clubtails have slightly separated but not "stalked" eyes.

Dragonflies also have three ocelli (the singular is ocellus), which are simple eyes on the top of the head. They sense differences in light intensity.

What range of light can dragonflies see?

Dragonflies can see the visible spectrum of light that we see. They can also see in the ultraviolet range and detect polarized light, as can many insects.

If dragonflies can see UV, what do they look like to each other?

There's quite a lot of information about what flower-visiting insects probably see because of their ability to perceive ultraviolet wavelengths. Some flowers, under UV light, have amazing runway lines leading to the source of nectar. These guidelines lead an insect towards yummy food—

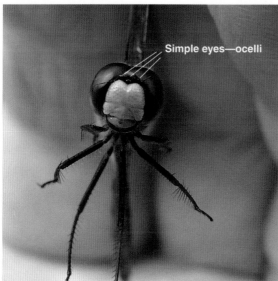

*Above: A clubtail's compound eyes do not meet in the middle, like on this Sulphur-tipped Clubtail (*Gomphus militaris*).*

*At right: Ocelli are simple eyes. See them on this White-faced Meadowhawk (*Sympetrum obtrusum*) in hand.*

and past stamens laden with pollen that rubs off on their backs. The insect gets a meal and the next flower the insect visits will be pollinated and set seed if it is the right species.

Dragonflies can see ultraviolet light, so it is fun to speculate what they might look like to each other. Is it possible the patterns and colors they sport might look quite different seen in the ultraviolet range? Would we still recognize them? So far, I have not found an answer to this question. A British study in 2011 captured images of dragonflies using equipment that filtered out all but UV light. In these conditions, different colors popped out and the sexes varied in UV reflectance, but overall, the experiments didn't show anything dramatic enough to suggest this appearance under ultraviolet plays an overwhelming role in species and sexual recognition.

Can dragonflies hear well?

If you think of hearing in the way we understand it, such as listening to jazz or Mozart or the human voice, then the answer is no. Dragonfly larvae, especially those that sprawl among vegetation mats or burrow in the mud, sand, or silt, have **mechanoreceptors** in their antennae and in their fore- and midlegs that are sensitive to touch, pressure changes, and vibrations. These mechanoreceptors sense prey movement and track small amplitude pressure waves in the water that suggest prey approach or predator danger.

Adult dragonflies have mechanoreceptors, too, that supplement their vision. The mechanoreceptors play a role in enabling the dragonfly to maintain flight stability or a horizontal posture and so on.

Do dragonflies have a good sense of smell?

Dragonflies have chemoreceptors that respond to chemical signals, but their range of ability to smell in the way we typically understand it isn't fully understood.

Do dragonflies communicate with pheromones?

Dragonflies are highly visual. They rely on their exceptional eyesight, not chemical attractants, to find mates.

You might guess this by noting how tiny dragonflies' antennae are. Insects, such as butterflies, moths, lacewings, and scorpion flies that use **pheromones** to signal to prospective mates, typically have more elaborate and sensitive antennae to pick up wafting odors.

*Is it fur? Not quite, but some dragonflies have plentiful body bristles: Four-spotted Skimmer (*Libellula quadrimaculata*).*

Do dragonflies have fur?

Dragonflies don't have fur in the sense we understand the silky fur of mammals. Some do have copious bristles growing from the surface of the thorax that can look like fur, but I don't know how effective they are as insulation. These bristles are sensitive to touch.

What do the segments on a dragonfly's abdomen signify?

A dragonfly's entire body is segmented—that's part of what characterizes arthropods. Dragonflies evolved from segmented ancestors. This is reflected in their present body form. You can see and appreciate the segmented character of a dragonfly most clearly in the abdomen.

The abdomen has ten segments, and in textbooks and field guides they are numbered for ease of description. The segment nearest to the thorax is S1. The rest are numbered from there to the tip, or S10. The last segment carries tail-tip structures called abdominal appendages. The segments are not of equal size. S1 and S10 are smaller. Very often the segments are not of a single color or pattern, which is an important feature in identification.

Segments S2 and S3 tend to be rounded and swollen in males. The underside of these segments is where the male stores his sperm just before mating. He also has a hook-like organ there to dislodge any alien sperm that the female may carry from a previous sexual encounter. His ability to remove or effectively overlay and disable his rival's sperm is said to give him a "last male advantage."

Females have their sex organs underneath S8, including a genital opening with a cover that might be a simple genital pore, or it might be developed into an **ovipositor**—an egg-laying organ. Sometimes, the sexual equipment will stick out like the proverbial sore thumb and be a great hint to identification.

The terminal appendages are different in adult dragonflies and damselflies and different between the sexes of each. This is why the appendages are often crucial in identification.

Dragonfly males have three anal appendages: two cerci (upper appendages) and one **epiproct** (lower appendage). These forceps-like appendages seize the female by the back of her head during mating. Ouch! Sometimes, captured female dragonflies have visible dents on the eye-surface where a male got overzealous. Dragonfly females may have cerci of various shapes and sizes, but they are not developed for grabbing. Females frequently seem to have broken-off cerci. Maybe they get in the way of mating?

Damselfly males have a similar abdominal anatomy to dragonflies, except that they have two pairs of appendages: two cerci (upper) and two **paraprocts** (lower) that form a clamp for seizing and holding the female.

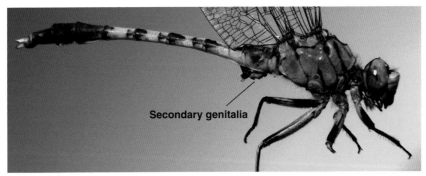

A male transfers and stores his sperm below his abdomen at S2–S3. The secondary genitalia include a hook-like organ to remove sperm from a previous mating from the female's body.

*The female Autumn Meadowhawk (*Sympetrum vicinum*) has a "sore-thumb" subgenital plate that sticks out.*

In many species these are uniquely shaped and a part of a lock and key mechanism between the male abdominal organs and the top front portion of the female's thorax called the mesostigmal plate. This lock and key system mostly prevents couplings between the wrong species.

In all cases, these details of abdominal anatomy provide vital clues to aid identification.

What are a dragonfly's legs like?

Each of a dragonfly's six legs, which originate on the thorax, is jointed and has a shell made of chitin. Each individual leg has two short and chunky upward-angled segments near the body called the coxa and the trochanter. Next come two long segments, the femur and tibia, that meet at the insect equivalent of an elbow. The last leg segment, or tarsus, is a foot equivalent and has a pair of tarsal claws at the end. Because of the unique forward tilt of the dragonfly's thorax, the legs are also angled forward. This ideal leg design works well for what a dragonfly needs to do.

Dragonfly and damselfly abdomen tips are crucial in identification.

Why do many dragonflies have hairy legs?

Many dragonflies have bristly spines on their legs that serve various purposes. The spines together can form a kind of basket to capture and hold large prey. Because a dragonfly's legs tilt forward on the thorax, they are ideally suited to capturing prey and perching, but they are not as well-suited for walking on the level. Why would they walk anyway, when they are such masters of flight? The spines on the legs help the dragonfly keep hold of prey—or sometimes a mate—or may even come in handy as weapons in confrontations with other odonates.

Hairy legs of a Halloween Pennant (Celithemis eponina*).*

Can dragonflies climb up windows as flies do?

I've never seen a dragonfly climb up a window. House flies can climb because the bases of their feet have a multitude of microscopic bristles, which can grip even the tiniest irregularities on any surface. On really slick surfaces, like glass, the flies use the adhesive action of these hairs, which are located on sticky pads on their tarsi (insect toe segments). Dragonflies have clawed tarsi, but they are not sticky like a house fly's tarsi.

However, dragonflies can climb with their tarsal claws on bumpy surfaces. I have seen **exuviae** (the shed larval shells of dragonflies) still attached high up on the screened porch of a lake-side cabin where the larvae had crawled many meters from the lake and then up an Everest-high mesh screen prior to emergence.

How many legs do dragonfly larvae have?

Dragonfly larvae have six legs, just as the adults do. In body form the larvae are obvious precursors to the adults, but they lack developed wings. Despite this, you can see prominent wing buds in the later larval stages. The main differences are that they have distinct abdominal appendages as adults, quite different from the dragonfly larva's spines or the damselfly larva's three external, paddle-shaped gills, which are not present in the adults.

How do dragonflies breathe?

The hemolymph (blood) of dragonflies plays little or no part in oxygen exchange. Water-dwelling larval dragonflies and damselflies breathe through gills. The gills of damselflies are made up of the three leaf-like structures at the end of the abdomen as well as some folds inside the rectum.

In dragonflies there are no outer gill structures, only folds inside the rectum over which water moves in and out. This also enables the larval dragonflies to employ a nifty means of escape. They jet away from danger with a rapid squirt of water from the rectum.

Adult odonates breathe through small holes in the body's external surface called spiracles. The spiracles connect with a system of tubes (trachea) that in turn lead to small, branched tubes with closed ends (tracheoles). The tracheoles spread into the body tissues and around individual cells allowing oxygen to diffuse in and carbon dioxide to diffuse out. Trachea and tracheoles are strengthened with spirals of cuticle to prevent their collapse. It's somewhat like spiral reinforcing you find in the hoses of drier vents, except on a truly microscopic scale. Watch carefully, and you can sometimes see a dragonfly's abdomen pulsating to help the process of gas exchange.

Damselfly larva with three paddle-like gills. JAMES BAILEY

Do dragonflies have blood?

Dragonflies have a blood equivalent, which is called hemolymph. This almost clear fluid is a bit like our blood plasma. It contains variable amounts and proportions of dissolved salts, sugars, proteins, and hormones and helps regulate the balance of water and salt in the body. It circulates in an open system with one main **dorsal** blood vessel that has valves towards the tail end that act as a pump, and it has uncontained circulation through the insect's body cavity.

Hemolymph performs a vital skeletal function. During the final molt, hemolymph is pumped into the veins of the crumpled wings and expands them to flight readiness. Once the wings have hardened, the hemolymph drains out again, leaving hollow wing veins that act like airplane struts to strengthen the wings.

Hemolymph is usually at low pressure in the insect's body, but the internal pressure can be increased when muscles contract. The internal pressure increases even more when the insect swallows air. This causes the gut to expand and to take up more space in the body cavity, creating pressure. It is this pressure that enables the insect to split a too-tight exoskeleton open at molting and helps prevent the soft body of a molting larva from losing its shape.

Does a dragonfly have a heart?

A dragonfly has a heart of sorts. The heart consists of a section of the main dorsal blood vessel divided by valves that pump the hemolymph forward in waves. The rest of the circulatory system is open, bathing the tissues with insect blood. The whole system normally works at fairly low pressure.

Do dragonflies pee and poop?

In words of Taro Gomi's famous book for toddlers—*Everyone Poops*. Dragonflies are no exception. The primary excretory system consists of hollow tubes called Malpighian tubules at the end of the hind gut. These tubules remove nitrogenous waste and various salts from the hemolymph (bug blood). Before adults expel any waste, much of the water is re-absorbed—losing lots of water is not in the body's best interest. So what you might see is a pasty or sludgy residue. Dry insect poop is termed frass.

Poop

*The scoop on poop: Variable Darner (*Aeshna interrupta*).*

In larvae, who breathe through their rectums, you might wonder whether incoming air becomes contaminated by body waste. In fact, the waste is packaged in a membrane, what author Cynthia Berger in *Wildguide: Dragonflies* calls an "organic garbage bag," which is expelled, sometimes explosively. These convenient little packets can provide scientists with clues to the larval diet.

What kind of brains do dragonflies have, and can they learn?

A dragonfly's brain consists of a cluster of nerve cells just above the esophagus. It's divided into three parts: one in control of the eyes and ocelli, one in control of antennae and the olfactory sense, and one responsible for the nerves from the front of the head. Not surprising in highly visual insects, roughly 80 percent of the brain is used for processing information to do with seeing.

In addition to processing sensory information that enables the dragonfly to function in its highly visual world, the brain seems to perform other actions innately. Dragonflies can catch prey by "knowing" the trajectory of a flying insect well enough to intercept it. They also seem to show selective attention—they tune out some prey items when they have started to pursue an insect on which they've set their sights. They can navigate, or at least travel long distances with the help of weather fronts to reach destinations during migration. They congregate in places of ample prey, but whether this is because they see the swarms of prey or because they see the mass gathering of other dragonflies would be hard to establish.

Typically among social insects, younger ones learn by following the lead of older individuals. Experiments with honeybees show they can learn (by trial and error) to come for sugar water placed in a clear dish above a marked sign, such as an X, and leave alone a similar dish of plain water that lies over a different symbol, such as a triangle. Then, if the dishes are switched, the bees will come to the X-marked spot, which is now plain water. The implication is that in the first part of the trial the bees learned to associate the X with food.

I have not been able to find any equivalent experiments with dragonflies. None of the abilities dragonflies exhibit imply actual learning, but this does not necessarily mean that they can't learn. So can they learn? The answer is, I don't know.

Do adult dragonfly males and females look the same?

Adult dragonfly male and females do not look the same. They look very different for two reasons.

Anatomically speaking, they are polar opposites. Some of these differences are obvious enough without close inspection (with many species you do need close inspection in order to identify them).

Damselfly males have four abdominal appendages: two cerci (claspers) and two paraprocts, which together are the apparatus for grabbing on to the female. Often the appendages are shaped to fit, lock and key fashion, with the female (see page 22). Males also have sex organs underneath abdominal segments S2–S3, which may cause a slight bulge in that area, best seen in side view.

Dragonfly males have three abdominal appendages: two cerci (claspers) and an epiproct that together form a three-pronged fork for grasping the female. The sexual organs underneath segments two and three often form a bulge. Males of both dragonflies and damselflies transfer sperm via a penis on segment S9 to the sperm repository beneath his segment S2-S3, so that the females are able to collect it from there.

Females of both groups have cerci, which are sometimes quite small. The cerci of female darners are sometimes damaged or missing because they seem to break off during mating. Females have genital pores under the end of the abdomen and some females have ovipositors, tubes through which they can insert their eggs into plant material (see page 22).

In the case of both dragonflies and damselflies, adult males and females may show major differences in color and pattern. In other words, they may be **dimorphic** (two-formed). In some species males and females look so radically different that they might be mistaken for two separate species.

Damselflies take this one step further. Females in some species have more than one color form. The first form resembles the male, and those females are called **andromorphs**. They are bright and look like the male damselfly of their species. The second form of females are called **heteromorphs**. They usually have duller coloring than the males. Some species have even more female forms!

*Two color forms of the Familiar Bluet (*Enallagma civile*)—a blue male and a brown (heteromorph) female.*

Male Widow Skimmer (Libellula luctuosa) *with "black next to the heart" (mourning).*

A female Widow Skimmer is unlike the male, lacking white on the wings.

Why can dragonflies of the same species vary in size as adults?

Once a dragonfly emerges and its exoskeleton hardens for flight, it doesn't continue to grow. And yet you may find adults of the same species and same sex vary in size. Often dragonflies that appear later in the season are a different size than the dragonflies from the early hatches. Size doesn't indicate the age of the dragonfly—small doesn't mean young. Instead, size depends on the circumstances in which the dragonfly spent its larval days.

Larvae go through a number of molts—anywhere from eight to fourteen—before they reach the preemergent **instar** (a name for the period between two molts). If the conditions of water temperature and day length are right when the larvae reach the preemergent instar stage, they will emerge. But that doesn't necessarily mean they've grown to a specific size. With less-than-ideal food supplies or water conditions, a larva may reach emergence as a runt and will forever be at the small end of the size spectrum.

Do adult dragonflies change their appearance as they age?

When dragonflies first emerge, they are known as **tenerals**. Teneral dragonflies are translucent and scarcely colored at all. They may be brownish or yellowish in hue. As they expand their wings and make their first flights, they often have a shimmering, milky look. As they develop, immature males often resemble the females in coloring. It is only later that both sexes develop their full adult coloration. You might think of them like birds coming into breeding plumage.

Some species—and this is more common in males than females—become coated with a white, blue, or gray waxy secretion from the cuticle. When dragonflies have this waxy coating, they are said to be **pruinose**. Pruinosity may help reduce water loss from a dragonfly's body and may reflect UV light (is it like sun block, I wonder?). The dragonfly can almost look as if it had been dipped in powdered sugar like Turkish delight. Pruinose males lose some of this waxy coating if the females grab them roughly during the mating process or just from daily life and flight. As for the dragonfly equivalent of gray hair and wrinkles, that manifests in tattered wings and, sometimes, missing legs.

A Common Whitetail *(*Plathemis lydia*) with a pruinose or waxy-coated abdomen.*

What makes a dragonfly's color?

You can't watch dragonflies and damselflies for very long without being amazed and delighted by their stunning and vibrant colors. As a stumbling poet-wannabe, I've tried to find words: iridescent gems, scraps of sky darting through summer, scarlet fly-by-days, or maybe streaks of azure capturing the eye.

Color, shimmer, dazzle, startle—words just don't do dragonflies justice. The colors are partly the outcome of vivid pigments and partly the outcome of the way body structure reflects some light selectively and absorbs the rest. Pigments account for the reds, yellows, browns, and blacks. The microscopic structure of the cuticle accounts for blues and iridescence. Greens seem to be a combination of colors—artist's-palette blends between yellow pigments and reflection of blue light.

Color is not the same for a dragonfly's entire life cycle, either. First, it develops gradually after emergence and reaches its most vivid state in sexual maturity. Sometimes, the natural color is overlaid with pruinosity—waxy coating that's produced by the cuticle—so adults, more often males, look bluish, whitish, or grayish and a little powdery (see page 31). This coating sometimes rubs off in the same way bloom can be wiped from plums.

*Color, shimmer, dazzle, startle . . . Neon Skimmer (*Libellula croceipennis*).*

One other factor plays into a dragonfly's color. Some species turn drab with cold, so if you are hunting for odes in early morning, you might overlook those dull gray damsels whose vibrant blue will catch your eye later in the day. This darkening and dulling of color may have a couple of benefits. First, it makes the dragonfly much less conspicuous as it roosts and so less vulnerable to predators. Second, a darker color absorbs ambient heat more effectively, allowing the dragonfly to fly at sunup as efficiently as possible. Later, the dull color would absorb too much heat at midday. The bright colors pay off by both minimizing overheating and attracting the opposite sex.

Do dragonflies keep their color after they die?

Dragonflies that die naturally do not long keep their colors. You may sometimes find a newly dead and still beautifully colored specimen. Make the most of the study opportunity. If you are unlucky enough to drive through a dragonfly swarm and inadvertently catch one or two in the automobile grill, chances are they'll be blackened by the time you find them. Still, even dead dragonflies can be worthy of a good look for the wing veins and the body shape and details.

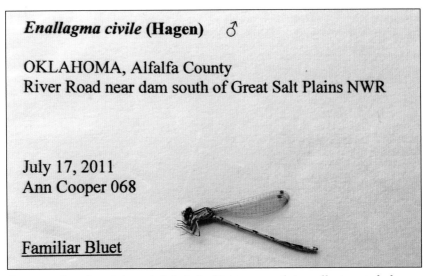

Enallagma civile (Hagen)　♂

OKLAHOMA, Alfalfa County
River Road near dam south of Great Salt Plains NWR

July 17, 2011
Ann Cooper 068

<u>Familiar Bluet</u>

A prepared study specimen is labeled with its name, date, collector, and place of capture.

People who collect dragonflies for scientific collections go to great lengths to preserve the color by immersing the insects in acetone, which kills them instantly and absorbs their body fat so the colors don't deteriorate. Museums present the collected insects in individual envelopes, wings folded, with all the necessary details of identification, location, date of capture, and collector, as well as any relevant ecological information. The specimens are housed in special insect-proof filing cabinets because even dead dragonflies are prey for the still living insects that can be a scourge of museum collections. Scientists can access these specimens many decades (or even centuries) after their collection. They are crucial for research, but rarely as beautiful to behold as live dragonflies.

Why do structural colors fade?

Structural colors are those formed when light reflects off the cellular configuration of the body surface of a dragonfly. These colors will fade in death if the underlying cells shrivel, distort, and no longer reflect light in the same way they did in life.

What are a dragonfly's wings made of?

A dragonfly's two pairs of long wings are made of two flattened layers of chitin, often transparent (sometimes faintly amber or variously patterned), surrounding a complex network of veins. The wing veins develop from the trachea present in the larval wing buds. At emergence, hemolymph is pumped into the wing veins, expanding them to give shape to the wings. The leading edges of the wings are rigid, but the trailing edges are more flexible to allow the wing actions necessary for flight. Once the wings harden, the hemolymph drains and the hollow veins form the struts that strengthen the wings.

Wing veins are intricate and functional, and they're also a key to identification in some species. Over the years, scientists have devised several systems of naming these veins. Look at any odonate textbook, and you can find wing diagrams pointing out the various named features. Or find a stray dragonfly wing on a pond bank and marvel at its fine and functional veins.

How strong are dragonfly wings?

Dragonfly wings look frail and gauzy, but that is deceptive. They may look like flat scraps of cellophane wrapping—I've been fooled this way when I've found detached wings along a shoreline—but they have complex structure.

In many species, the wings are long compared to their width (in other words, they have a high aspect ratio). This indicates effective long-distance flight potential. In cross section the wings look crinkly and corrugated—not flat at all. This 3-D surface makes for strength, stiffness, and stability. Look up close, and you'll see that the veins form an intricate structural network (incidentally, also important in species identification). The small cell towards the tip of the leading edge of each wing, called the **pterostigma**, functions as a damper to reduce wing flutter and increase efficiency as the dragonfly flaps its wings. The node, or midpoint of the leading edge of the wing, is a point where the wing can twist to create the appropriate wing shape to pull off specific flight maneuvers.

At the microscopic level, the wing surfaces have water-repellant structures that help prevent water droplet buildup that would interfere with flight aerodynamics.

*Delicate tracery of wing veins: Roseate Skimmer (*Orthemis ferruginea*).*

Pterostigmas and nodes show up well in the wings of the Great Blue Skimmer (Libellula vibrans).

How do dragonflies fly?

Dragonflies have no links between their four wings, and each wing can move independently. In studies of tethered dragonflies flying in wind tunnels, scientists tracked turbulence by watching what happened to smoke around the moving wings. It turned out that dragonflies twist their wings on the downstroke, which causes mini whirlwinds to move air faster over the upper wing surface. This acts to reduce pressure and increase lift.

During hovering, a dragonfly's body keeps close to horizontal at all times. The wings push backwards and downwards until the end of the stroke, when they feather upwards and come forwards. Z. Jane Wang of Cornell University described the flight in these terms: "The dragonfly's asymmetric rowing motion allows it to support much of its weight by the upward drag created during the down stroke." Dragonflies also turn in flight by feathering the wings on the inside of the turn in a rowing-like action.

Another interesting feature of dragonfly flight is its variability. The dragonfly may flap its wings in phase, something it often does on takeoff, which gives it a power burst and maximum lift. Or it may flap its wings out of phase, which it does when hovering, so it can stay airborne with less expenditure of effort because of the aerodynamic interaction between the contra-beating wings.

How fast do dragonfly wings beat?

Dragonflies' wings appear to beat fast and sometimes, especially in the case of large darners, you can hear the wing-rattle as they fly past or come in to roost. The fact that a dragonfly's four wings work independently and frequently beat out of phase helps create the impression of blur. Scientists believe this type of wing action is more primitive than the wing action produced with linked wings, but it works.

A whole subset of research focuses on wing beat kinematics and the analysis of odonate flight, measured in flight cages or in the wild. In general, dragonflies seem to have modest wing beat frequency (damselflies more so). As for numbers, some measured members of the genus *Aeshna* (Mosaic Darners) clock in at 22–28 beats per second. Compare this with male mosquitoes buzzing away at more than 550 beats per second.

For another comparison, hummingbirds seem to have wing beat frequencies in the range of 22–78 beats per second.

Can dragonflies fly backwards?

Yes, dragonflies may fly backwards for short distances. It's those four amazing, independently beating wings at work again.

How fast can dragonflies fly?

Studies tracking dragonflies in flight suggest that they can fly more than 40 miles per hour when necessary. Most of the time, they are slower than that. Some dragonflies are capable of such slow flight you'd expect them to stall. Damselflies, on average, are slow fliers, probably moving, at most, about 6 miles per hour.

What happens if a dragonfly's wings are damaged?

Dragonflies are able to survive even after suffering extensive damage to their wings, or even loss of one of them. You will sometimes see severely injured dragonflies still flying. What you don't see is all those others with similar wing damage that became predator food.

An end-of-season dragonfly with damaged hindwings: Four-spotted Skimmer.

Wing damage has several consequences. It alters the lift the wings are capable of generating, so that takeoff is slowed. It reduces the speed at which the insect can fly, making it more vulnerable to predation and less able to catch its own prey. There is no way, once damaged, the wings can regrow or repair themselves.

Record Holders

What is the largest dragonfly in the world?

The largest odonate known in the world today is a damselfly. It lives in wet forests in Central and South America, and its wingspan can reach 190 millimeters (7½ inches). Its name is *Megaloprepus coerulatus*, the Blue Helicopter Damsel, and it belongs in the Forest Giant family. It eats mostly spiders. It is long and slender, and it has stunning white and black wing tips. The Blue Helicopter Damsel is truly eye-catching as it flutters across a forest clearing, with its patterned, windmill-blade wings. I recently saw this species for the first time. Amazing!

There's no complete agreement on the largest dragonfly. Some people think that the Giant Hawaiian Darner, *Anax strenuus*, with a wingspan 150 millimeters (over 6 inches), is the largest. It looks superficially like the Common Green Darner. Others claim the Giant Petaltail of northeastern Australia, *Petalura ingentissima*, takes the record. Its wingspan has been recorded at 160 millimeters (6.3 inches).

If you search for such information, it's always difficult to establish hard and fast numbers as different sources offer different answers. So take these figures with a grain of skepticism. What I always want to know is who gets the job of measuring—and do they want an assistant?

What is the smallest dragonfly in the world?

The smallest dragonfly in the world is said to be the Northern Pygmyfly, *Nannophya pygmaea*, which lives in eastern Asia. It's only about 15 millimeters (0.6 inches) long and has a wingspan of about 20 millimeters (0.8 inches). It is endangered.

The smallest damselflies may be tiny fliers in the genus *Agriocnemis*. Among them is *Agriocnemis pygmaea*, which is variously called Pygmy Dartlet, Wandering Wisp, Wandering Midget, or Pygmy Wisp; what wonderfully evocative names! These "Wisps"—that really is their generic common name—belong with the Pond Damsels. The smaller ones are barely 19 millimeters (0.75 inch) in wingspan.

What is the largest dragonfly in the United States?

The largest dragonfly in the United States is the Giant Darner, *Anax walsinghami*, which grows to 127 millimeters (5 inches) long and 127 millimeters (5 inches) wingspan. All I know is that this elegant, spindly insect seems huge when it zips by a dragonfly fancier sitting on a rock beside a trickling desert wash.

The largest damselfly in the United States, the Great Spreadwing (*Archilestes grandis*) is a common late-season spreadwing with stunning blue eyes. I'm happy to have these hatching from my garden pond.

Again, I caution you against taking these numbers as definitive. When it comes to measurements, it depends on the particular specimen in hand that is being measured. The field guide I rely on, *Dragonflies and Damselflies of the West* by Dennis Paulson, gives two size stats: TL (total length) and HW (hindwing). Both of these stats include a range of measurement to account for variability between sexes and among individuals of the species. For example, the Giant Spreadwing is "TL 50–62 mm and HW 31–40 mm." That's enough difference between the smallest and largest specimens to easily account for differences in opinion on the world record holders.

What is the smallest dragonfly in North America?

The Elfin Skimmer (*Nannothemis bella*) is the smallest North American dragonfly, although, Dennis Paulson aptly says in *Dragonflies of Eastern North America*, that the Elfin skimmer is "barely big enough to be called a dragon."

Above: Smallest dragonfly in North America: Elfin Skimmer. It is "barely big enough to be called a dragon," according to Dennis Paulson. DAVID REED
On previous page: Largest dragonfly in North America: Giant Darner.
TRIPP DAVENPORT

The smallest damselfly is probably the extremely common Citrine Forktail (*Ischnura hastata*), whose wingspan can be as little as 18 millimeters (0.7 inch). These flit low in the grasses and are colored like dry grass stems, so they are easy to overlook.

How much does a dragonfly weigh?

A dragonfly doesn't weigh very much. A dime weighs about 2 grams. A single M&M weighs less than a gram (actually, about 0.85 grams—I weighed them before I ate them). The smallest dragonflies weigh about 0.003 grams (0.0001 ounce)—a fraction of one M&M. The largest ones weigh around 3 grams (0.1 ounce). Imagine, a mid sized dragonfly tips the scale at three M&Ms or one dime—just a tiny scrap of feistiness.

Dragonfly Lifestyles

Do dragonflies live everywhere?

Dragonflies live on every continent except Antarctica. They may not be found on all small or isolated islands or in barren deserts, but with their strong flight they are adept at dispersal. They require wet, or at least moist, habitats for the egg and larval stages of their lives as well as for meeting and mating. However, they can be found in areas quite distant from bodies of water during some life stages, notably when they are not yet sexually mature, when they are part of feeding swarms, or when they are in the process of migrating.

A small number of dragonflies are terrestrial throughout their lives. The larvae live in burrows in damp mud or moss, or in the splash zone of springs and the mud of seeps. Some eggs even survive on dry land for varying periods before dampness arrives and permits growth to proceed. These dragonflies are the exception.

What kind of watery habitats do dragonflies inhabit?

Dragonflies use virtually all freshwater habitats that they can find, and some brackish water habitats, too. Their larvae do not live in the ocean. Different species have their own preferred habitats: ponds, rivers, streams, canals, ditches, puddles, stock tanks, swamps, marshes, fens, seeps, springs, alkaline playas, brackish tidal reaches, tree holes in forest clearings, and even pockets of water in leaf axils of plants such as tropical bromeliads.

Tamarack Pond, Colorado: rare water amid desert, weedy banks, and cattails makes a promising habitat.

Dragonflies can expand their breeding territories by seeking out and colonizing likely-looking wetlands of the type they favor. Imagine a dragonfly flying high, looking for reflective bodies of water, and you can understand how it could make a mistake. A glistening holding pond of toxic stew, or an oil slick, or even the La Brea Tar Pits could look promising—until it was too late to back off.

What makes a good dragonfly habitat?

Any area that fulfills certain requirements can be a good dragonfly habitat. It has to satisfy the needs of dragonflies at all stages of their lives—both larval and adult. This usually means clean enough water for egg-laying and larval development and nearby places for adults to feed, roost, and mate.

What is meant by the terms fliers and perchers?

Some species of dragonflies spend almost all their active time in flight. These strong, direct fliers rarely perch except when they are tenerals, or when they roost—or sometimes when they mate. These are called fliers

The Twelve-spotted Skimmer, a percher, returns to the same twig again and again.

and the Common Green Darner is representative of them. They typically eat on the wing.

Other species of dragonflies spend most of their active time perching on waterside vegetation, snags, or rocks, and they only take flights to protect territory, chase down mates, or feed. The Twelve-spotted Skimmer, *Libellula pulchella*, is a typical percher.

The perchers may be the easiest dragonflies to get to know up close and personal, as they return to their favorite perches reliably enough to be great photo subjects!

Are all dragonflies predators?

Dragonflies and damselflies are all ferocious predators, both as larvae and as adults. Larvae prey on whatever small animals they can find and capture. When they're small, they live on microscopic pond creatures—copepods, crustaceans, and the larvae of aquatic insects. As they grow, dragonfly larvae are able to capture larger prey, such as the larvae of midges, blackflies, mosquitoes, and small worms. By the time they're full size, they may catch large worms and aquatic insects (even the larvae of other dragonflies), tiny fish, and tadpoles.

Adult dragonflies are opportunists. They feed on a wide variety of insects depending on what they can find, including midges, mosquitoes, mayflies, flies, bees, ants, beetles, and butterflies. They will readily eat other dragonflies and damselflies. They take advantage of mayfly hatches and the flying stage of ants and termites. There have even been a few documented cases of large dragonflies catching small hummingbirds. This may have been accidental (mistaken identity?), and hummingbirds are certainly not a standard food source for dragonflies.

Dragonflies are not merely predators—they are among the most efficient predators in the animal kingdom. One study showed these aerial killers succeeded in capturing their target prey more than 95 percent of the time, although I don't know if this study depended on an artificially steady and profuse supply of edible insects. The rate achieved certainly beats the record of the African lion, which is successful on about one chase in four.

How do dragonflies catch their food?

Larval dragonflies hunt in the water, sometimes by ambush and sometimes by stalking. They spot prey by sight or by feeling vibrations. Their capture mechanism for prey is a marvel of specialization. The larva has a hinged lower lip, or **labium**, that is normally folded against the face, almost like a mask. This lip can be flat or spoon-shaped depending on species and has moveable spikes on the front edge that are a little like tines of a fork. With lighting speed, the labium shoots out to capture prey. When the labium is pulled back again, the prey is neatly enfolded inside.

Above: A dragonfly larva caught with its spoon-like labium extended.
At left: A Familiar Bluet enjoys a meal of deerfly.

Small larvae catch tiny prey; larger larvae—late instars—go for big meals such as larger insects and their larvae, small fish, or tadpoles. Strangely, voracious dragonfly larvae may be partly responsible for an unsolved environmental mystery. You may have read reports of people finding legless or partially-deformed frogs and wondered what caused them. We may imagine many environmental scenarios: pollution, pesticides, parasites, the global amphibian decline, UV radiation, ozone depletion, or something else? Turns out that at least some of the damage might be entirely natural. When a large odonate larva captures a tadpole, it turns it around to find the first bite. The newly-budding hind limbs are easy first morsels to grasp. If the tadpole escapes before the next snip, it may survive three-legged.

Adult dragonflies capture prey on the wing. They grab small prey with their mandibles and gulp it down as they go. Larger prey offers a greater challenge. The dragonflies may need to use their long legs to help seize, hold, and subdue their prey. The forelegs, often bearing stiff bristles, form very effective baskets (see page 59). A dragonfly may retire to a perch while it comes to grips with its lavish feast. It may discard remnants left over from a beetle or butterfly meal—wings or other hard parts with minimal food value.

Recent research shows that dragonflies do not hunt randomly. Dragonflies are known to track a moving target and calculate its trajectory so that the dragonfly can intercept it. This is accomplished with a master circuit of only sixteen neurons! Dragonflies also seem to have the capacity to lock on to one prey item in a swarm and go for it, while ignoring other distracting flybys. In humans, the ability to block out one thing while focusing on another (as we do with party conversations) is called selective attention. Australian scientists recently demonstrated selective attention was really happening by probing single neurons in a dragonfly's brain with minute electrodes about 1/1500th the width of human hairs and monitoring the electrical responses to prey items in the dragonfly's visual field. Amazing!

Do dragonflies eat as they fly?

Yes, if the prey is small enough to handle in flight, dragonflies will eat as they go. Fast food? Some dragonflies routinely perch while they eat larger morsels.

I can find no evidence to suggest red dragonflies are poisonous or noxious to animals that prey on them. Their bodies do not generate poisons. They do not eat plants that enable them to sequester toxins in the way that Monarch Butterfly caterpillars ingest the toxic sap of milkweed leaves. I suppose it might be possible for dragonflies to accumulate toxins in their own bodies if they ate enough brightly-colored toxin-containing bugs. But I believe this is unlikely to happen. Dragonflies are predatory generalists and so would be unlikely to consume enough of a single kind of toxic insect to accumulate a toxin-load.

Do dragonfly wing patches deflect predators, as butterfly "eyespots" do?

Many butterfly and moth species have wing markings that help them evade or survive a predator's attack. For example, red underwing moths are drab when perched. If they are threatened, they take off with a sudden flash of bright red under wings that often distracts a predator long enough for the moth to make its getaway.

Some butterflies have noticeable eyespots on their hindwings. These fake eyes may mimic something watching—the stunning Owl Butterfly makes many predators think twice about attacking. Or the eyespots may mimic real eyes so that a predatory bird pecks at the fake eyes and the real eyes at the head end are spared. In this case, the butterfly lives to flutter another day, albeit with tattered wings that reduce its flight fitness.

So do dragonfly wing patches serve any of these functions? The colored wing splotches and bands that some dragonfly species have are certainly handy to us as a means of identifying them. Of course, they also help male or female members of a species to recognize each other. I've wondered if wing coloration helps break up the outline and renders the insect less obvious to predators or less visible to prey. This seems a stretch to me because if the patterns catch my eyes, why wouldn't they catch the eyes of predators?

No doubt, when a dragonfly is trying to escape a predator, the whirling patterns on its fast-moving wings would be confusing and dazzling—almost hypnotic—to anything pursuing it. Imagine trying to follow the motion of a whirling pinwheel.

As for those species that carry vaguely eye-shaped wing dots, I have never seen specific wing damage in the areas of the spots as you frequently see on butterfly wings. That doesn't mean it doesn't happen . . . but yet again, I've generated a question that I can't answer!

*Eye-catching wing coloring: Calico Pennant (*Celithemis elisa*).*

Why do dragonflies hunt near traffic lights?

Do dragonflies hunt near traffic lights? This question is a pure flight of fancy. Often, when I am stopped at traffic lights I see dragonflies hawking for insects, along with swallows. Are there more insects—and therefore more predatory dragonflies—here than there are in other places?

I have wondered if the air quality in places where vehicles are idling is compromised to the extent that insects flying there are more sluggish and easier to capture. For sure, tailpipes emit some ghastly stuff: nitrogen oxide, volatile compounds that react with sunlight to make ozone, carbon monoxide, toxins such as benzene, particulates, and carbon dioxide. It's enough to make one breathless! I have also wondered if carbon dioxide draws in mosquitoes, which in turn attract dragonflies. But all evidence suggests that it's a combination of carbon dioxide and lactic acid given off by humans and other animals that draws in biting critters. Carbon dioxide alone is not so appealing.

Perhaps street lights attract insects that in turn draw in late-feeding birds and dragonflies.

Or am I just so hooked on odes that I'm inclined to notice them everywhere, especially when I'm stopped in traffic?

What dangers do dragonflies face?

Although dragonflies are predators, they are fairly small as far as predators go. So naturally they are vulnerable to larger predators—everything from birds and bats in the air to other insects, fish, frogs, snakes, and turtles in the water.

Beyond predation, the greatest hazards to dragonfly life are degradation of water quality and elimination of habitat. Some species of dragonfly thrive in less-than-pristine conditions where water may be tainted with agricultural runoff, excess fertilizers, or even trace pesticides. Other species tolerate only lakes and streams with clear water and no contamination of any kind. Anytime water quality changes it will change the balance of dragonfly species able to survive in that locale.

Habitat loss is even more serious over the long haul. In theory, contaminated water could be cleaned up and be available again as acceptable habitat. But once gone, the drained lake and channelized stream are lost forever. A dragonfly cannot escape these hazards if the hazards are sufficiently widespread.

When it comes to global climate change, all bets are off. We don't know in enough detail what will happen if we return to dust bowl type conditions in the Southwest or if spring comes earlier in the Northeast. It's possible that warming will cause expansion of dragonfly habitat towards the higher latitudes. It's also possible that species will be lost if extreme droughts become more frequent and wetland areas become parched.

How do dragonflies defend themselves?

Dragonflies do *not* sting. As larvae, their chief defense is camouflage when they lurk among pond vegetation, or a quick burst of speed away from danger when they are seen. Many odonate larvae are brown, green, or a blend of both and rely on a combination of immobility and cryptic coloring to stay safe. Other larvae burrow into the bottom mud leaving only their mouthparts and breathing tails exposed. Even so, the number of larvae that survive to achieve adulthood is a minute fraction of the total number of eggs laid. The death rate is high, especially in the early instars.

As adults, dragonflies rely on extreme speed and maneuverability as their best defense against predation. One-on-one with other odes, they are capable of fighting back by biting or by scrabbling with their clawed front feet.

This camouflaged larva blends in well with lichens on a twig.
ANATOTLICH/SHUTTERSTOCK.COM

When are dragonflies most active?

Dragonflies are most active on sunny days when the temperature is warm enough for them to be on the wing, but not so scorching hot that they retreat to hang up in the shade. The conventional wisdom is that you should go out and look for dragonflies from midmorning until mid to late afternoon, but it is also fun to go earlier and meet the dragonflies before they warm up, if you want to take photos. Unlike the sport of hot-shot birding, crack-of-dawn starts are not required.

As soon as it turns cloudy, windy, or above all, rainy, dragonfly and damselfly activity virtually ceases (although there are some tropical species that continue to hunt through rainy periods). Perhaps heavy cloud sends damselflies into night-mode, so they retreat to roosts to wait out storms. That makes sense for small, fragile creatures. After all, a raindrop hitting such a small body is not pleasant to contemplate. Windy days also offer meager dragonfly watching.

As for the time of year to go ode-hunting, it depends entirely where *you* hang out. In Colorado, various species of odes can be seen from late spring until the first severe frost. More southerly states have some species on the wing all year.

Are dragonflies active at night?

Dragonflies are primarily active by day—diurnal. However, this only tells part of the story.

Many adult dragonflies first emerge under cover of darkness. By the time it is light, enough time has passed for the newly emerged creature's exoskeleton to partially harden. It then takes its somewhat fluttery maiden flight to a place of safety away from the water and rests there until its flight capacity is fully functional. The virtue of this timetable is that the insects can hatch and leave the area before predators spot them.

Some dragonfly species are active in the late afternoon until dusk—or later. The Vesper Bluet (*Enallagma vesperum*) is one of them. You often become aware of them in numbers, eye-catching yellow matchsticks lying on lily pads, just as the light is beginning to fade.

Some dragonflies, for example the River Cruisers, actively patrol their river beat until dark. The Shadowdragons are known for hunting for about half an hour between sunset and near dark.

You may also see dragonflies, or hear the rattle of their wings, as they tuck into roosts around your dwelling, or if they are disturbed from those roosts after dark. Blue-eyed Darners and other darners will at times glean midges and other small insects that are attracted to porch lights, camp lanterns, and well-lit gas stations or stores, and so extend their feeding hours.

Where do dragonflies sleep?

Dragonflies roost at night, and sometimes in extreme daytime heat or stormy conditions, in the shade and shelter of vegetation. They may roost individually or clustered together. I have read that darners often hang up

in large swarms on the west side of trees, often quite high up. In the early morning they ease their way around to the east side of the roost to catch the morning rays. I have not been lucky enough to see this (yet). Live in hope!

Other dragonflies tuck into the shelter of reed beds or long grasses. Once, in Kansas, there seemed to be Widow Skimmers by the dozens

A Vesper Bluet perches on a lily pad in the slant light of sundown.

Widow Skimmers roosting low in the undergrowth.

hanging out in unmowed grass around a fishing lake only about a foot from the ground or from each other.

Damselflies may roost deep in the grass, too. As their colors often fade in the chill of night, the vivid blue turning to drab gray, they do not attract attention.

On damp, chilly nights these insects can become dotted with dew. I like to think that's where the inspiration for dragonfly jewelry originated.

How do dragonflies stay safe when they're roosting?

It's tempting to answer this question flippantly, knowing how hard it is to find roosting dragonflies when you are really looking for them! And anyway, how would you know how safe dragonflies are when they are roosting or what proportion of them is picked off by predators?

Many dragonflies on the wing are brightly colored—far from the standard idea of camouflage. But that's when they are zipping around or perched blatantly on a pond-bank plant. When they are tucked in among vegetation and motionless, they are easy to overlook.

When you look more carefully at patterns, you'll see that many multi-colored species, such as the darners, have mottled, broken-up patterns that

An Eastern Pondhawk spangled with early morning dew.

A Lake Darner (Aeshna eremita) *blends with the tree in which it roosts.*

serve them well among dappled light and shade. Other species are dark—bark colored, if you like—and blend beautifully with the tree trunks they rest on. Other species roost hanging perpendicular and look just like twigs of a bush or blades of grass.

Some species become duller colored in the cold, which makes them less noticeable while they roost at night. I can only suppose that the things making dragonflies hard for me to see probably have protective benefits against their natural predators, too.

How do dragonflies stay warm?

All insects, including odonates, are called **ectotherms**, or, more informally, "cold blooded" (not a scientific term). Simply stated, dragonflies will be warm when their surroundings are warm and cold when their surroundings are cold. They do not keep their body temperatures at a set point as mammals and birds do.

This is only part of the story. Dragonflies have various strategies to warm their bodies. They bask in the sun when it is chilly and frequently choose a heat absorbing surface on which to rest. You can often find odonates basking on gravel roads, wooden fences, or boardwalks soaking up some rays. They align their bodies to get the maximum solar gain.

Another strategy dragonflies use to warm up is shivering. Tiny muscular movements that rattle the wings also generate warmth to rev up the wing muscles for flight.

*A Variegated Meadowhawk (*Sympetrum corruptum*) warms up on a rock.*

On the subject of keeping things warm, scientists in Japan discovered that among male damselflies performing courtship displays in the sun, those that had the hottest bodies (as sensed by thermal imaging cameras) attracted more mates. They literally were "hot stuff." It's thought that hot males in sunny territories where eggs develop faster may have a superior reproductive success rate.

How do dragonflies stay warm in areas of cold winters?

The short answer is dragonflies don't stay warm during winter in cold regions. Adults of a few dragonfly species that live in high-latitude temperate regions migrate to warmer places where they can still find food. A few species, such as the Autumn Meadowhawk, can survive fairly low fall temperatures in late season by choosing perches carefully and altering their posture to minimize cooling. In the end, when winter comes, non-migrating, cold-climate dragonfly adults perish.

Larval dragonflies of species that live in chilly regions spend the winter in a state of suspended animation in their underwater habitats, as do many amphibians, reptiles, and fish. There they'll stay, scarcely moving or eating, and just biding their time. As the water warms in spring, the larvae become active again and carry on eating, growing, molting, and eventually transforming (metamorphosing) into adult dragonflies.

There's an advantage to spending the winter in a dormant or partially dormant state. It uses much less energy than we, as warm-blooded animals, need to use to survive the winter. The disadvantage is that it can take six or seven years for some dragonfly larvae to develop in very cold mountain streams.

How does a dragonfly keep from baking in the sun?

When the outside temperature soars, a dragonfly's body can get too hot. A dragonfly has several strategies it may use to prevent overheating. If it chooses to stay in the sun, the dragonfly will often align its body so as to minimize the sun's rays that fall directly on it. Sometimes this means perching in the obelisk position, with the abdomen pointing skywards and directly at the sun to minimize the surface area that receives direct sunlight. Other species perch with the abdomen drooping downwards to reduce the impact of direct sunlight.

*A Blue Dasher (*Pachydiplax longipennis*) rests in the obelisk position.*

It has also been suggested that the wing patches of some species may help keep the dragonfly cool by acting as directional sunshades to keep the most intense rays off the thoracic region.

In even more intense heat, the dragonfly may opt to hang up in the shade of trees or shrubs until things cool down again. Some dragonflies cool off with a quick dip in the water, losing body heat when the water evaporates.

Do dragonflies drink?

Adult dragonflies get a fair amount of water from the food they eat, which is 60 to 80 percent water. They supplement this metabolic water by drinking, but it's hard to know how much and how often they drink directly from the water surface, either in flight or by landing.

Dragonflies dip in the water at times to cool down. And some species dip underwater in the course of laying eggs. So you'd need a lot of researchers looking specifically at drinking dragonflies to get the whole picture.

Dragonflies are known to drink in captivity. They've been seen drinking from the water surface, sipping dew from early morning vegetation, and even carrying single droplets away from the water in their forelegs.

Contact guarding—the male will help haul the female out of the water.

but he must have managed to let go of his mate because a minute or so later he struggled to the surface and took off again.

For teneral (recently hatched) odonates, immersion is a different matter. Predators attack many of them before they can even dry their wings. Alternatively, their wings might fail to expand sufficiently to enable a frail maiden flight. And one wave from a passing speedboat can swamp these newly emerged insects. You can often find scores of damselflies that didn't make it, floating in the edges of a pond. They make good study subjects.

What are dragonflies doing when they go out and back from a perch by the pond?

Some dragonflies, especially the skimmers, occupy perches along pond or river banks and make irregular forays over the water, returning to the same, or a nearby, perch. The perchers (see page 44) are often males **guarding** territory they deem to be good habitat into which their eventual mates should lay eggs. These males may dart out and back to send off rivals that invade their territory. These rivals are commonly males of the same species, which threaten the supremacy of the resident male over available females in the vicinity. But a dragonfly may also leave its perch to fend off males of another species or to investigate potential mates of its own species. Territories are variable in size and may be held for a day or for certain hours of a day. They may also shrink under pressure from a large number of **conspecifics** (same species) active in the area.

Confrontations are like aerial dogfights and look more violent than they actually are. Chances are the resident males will threaten and send off a rival without direct physical action, although a male is quite capable of zooming up on a rival from below and making contact.

Males also might dart out from a perch to check out a prospective mate. If she seems receptive—and even sometimes when she doesn't— he will try to grab her by the back of the head and check her out. A male who maintains a promising territory ends up mating more successfully. The fringe males have fewer mating opportunities but take them when they can, often darting in when the main male is otherwise distracted.

With all this energy going towards meeting and mating and protecting turf, there is only a little time left over to grab food. This is another reason a male might foray out over the water. It's fun to wait and watch when you find a male with a relatively constant perch, and see if you can figure out what his forays signify. There's no better way to squander a hot afternoon in the marsh!

A confrontation between a Blue Dasher and a meadowhawk.

A female Common Green Darner lays eggs as the male contact guards her.

What are dragonflies doing when two together fly over the pond?

When two dragonflies fly "in formation"—that is, not chasing each other and not in contact either—they will generally be a mated female preparing to lay eggs being guarded by her most recent male. This is called **non-contact guarding**. In non-contact guarding, a male attempts to prevent his female from mating again before she has a chance to lay eggs. It's his paternity insurance. If the male gets carried away chasing off another male who gets too close, there's always the possibility that a third male may dart in to grab the female. It really is a bug-eat-bug mating scene.

Meanwhile, the female will often begin ovipositing (egg-laying), dipping her abdomen in the water to drop an egg, or maybe a few eggs at a time, in places right for her species. Some species lay on floating mats of vegetation, some lay in the warm shallows, and some spread eggs with apparent abandon over deeper areas of water. Check out the style of the dragonfly pairs you are watching.

How long can dragonflies stay underwater?

Many damselflies are able to spend time completely underwater in the course of laying eggs into plant material. Sometimes the male keeps a hold of his mate, and they submerge together. Other times he might wait at the surface, either perched or hovering, for her to reappear and may help her get airborne again.

Researchers have timed how long different species of damselflies can stay underwater. Some species remained submerged for between 30 minutes to an hour. Others submerged for even longer. There's even documentation that a Marsh Bluet (*Enallagma ebrium*) stayed underwater for five hours.

You might wonder how they can stay down so long. There's a good possibility that they take down bubbles of air with them and shield their forewings with their closed hindwings so the wings remain dry enough for the damsel to get out of the water again when she must.

Finding out how deep these laying females go is a challenge. And who knows if the presence of an observer skews the results? Written records suggest the depth can be as shallow as a centimeter or as deep as a meter. For dragonflies, complete submergence is a very rare happening.

How long do dragonflies live?

Many people, when they ask how long dragonflies live, are really asking how long the adult dragonflies they see flitting around the pond are likely to live if they make it to old age. Typically, the answer is anywhere from two to six weeks if they are lucky. Damselflies live a shorter time, some species for as short as two or three days.

This is just a ballpark number for temperate-zone dragonflies. Many adult dragonflies perish along the way. Mortality is high. Some dragonflies fail to emerge completely. They can be washed away by boat wakes, snapped up in the teneral (vulnerable) stage by frogs and snakes, or pecked off in midair by a passing flycatcher. Life is hard and then they die.

However, this number doesn't account for the whole life cycle. Dragonflies spend a great proportion of their lives as larvae living in the water. They pass through multiple growth stages, or instars, before they emerge. Some species go from egg to adult in one year. Others, especially cold-climate dragonflies, may take several years to complete the cycle, with most of that time (up to five years) spent underwater. Bearing this in mind, how long does a dragonfly live? The real answer is anywhere from weeks to years.

There's another complicating factor. When a life cycle takes place in several stages and in two distinct habitats (water and land), and in many possible ecological areas, there are numerous reasons why timing may

Where and how do dragonflies lay their eggs?

Dragonflies lay their eggs in water or in moist habitats. Some lay eggs in damp vegetation that floods seasonally. Others lay eggs above dry land and the eggs filter down to lie among tall grasses. Some species lay eggs in temporary puddles. Others even lay eggs in tree holes and small basins of water around tropical rainforest plants, such as bromeliads.

Some dragonfly females drop their eggs singly or in clusters in a seemingly random way as they fly above the water of their chosen ovipositing (egg-laying) site. Some periodically tap their abdomen tips on the water to release an egg or eggs as they fly over ponds or lakes. Yet others dip over and over again in the same small area of shallows. The eggs bubble out from a genital pore on the underside of the abdomen tip. In some species, the females actively flick the eggs away from their bodies while remaining high above the target water surface. That way, the adult is less likely to be snapped up by a water-based predator.

The eggs drift down into floating vegetation or the bottom silt. Immediately after laying, the eggs make a tasty snack for predators. After a while the eggs become more gelatinous—and less tasty? The whole sequence appears to be rather hit-and-miss, but it works.

Some species deposit eggs directly into the gravel or mud substrate of lakes and ponds. Dragonflies that deposit eggs in moving water sometimes have "sticky" eggs to help prevent the eggs from washing away.

A female skimmer with an egg mass at the tip of her abdomen.

Other odonates, including damselflies and some dragonflies (petaltails and darners) lay eggs directly into vegetation. In this case, they inject the eggs inside plant stems, tangles of waterweed, mats of algae, and even woody tissue, with the help of the female's ovipositor. This appendage is capable of making a small slit in the plant material through which the female stuffs the eggs into the protected cavity.

Egg-laying doesn't always go as intended. Dragonflies have been known to try and oviposit (lay eggs) on wet roads or even shiny car bodies, mistaking the glistening surface for water. Even more harrowing, darners have been known (extremely rarely) to try and inject an egg through a slit in human skin. Ouch!

How do dragonflies know where to lay their eggs?

Dragonflies use various visual clues to determine where in their habitat to lay eggs. When they look down on water, it seems that they see different reflective patterns depending on the depth of water, its clarity or murkiness, and the character of the bottom. This helps them find potential habitats. This is the result of polarized vision, which works in much the same way as the polarized sunglasses you might wear by a pond to see the details of pond life. Dragonflies are also able to see the outlines of floating plants and the character of the surrounding vegetation.

A few species drop eggs over territory that is dry but will be wet at some later time. How they determine what the future will bring is a mystery. Maybe they can tell there's no tall vegetation and see remnant puddles, brown as they may be, that hint at wetland potential. For sure, they can see reflections bouncing from any water body, however small. But dragonflies can be deceived by reflections off shiny car bodies or wet roads (see above).

How long does a dragonfly stay as an egg?

A dragonfly can stay in the egg stage for a matter of days if it completes its life cycle quickly. This may happen if the eggs are laid in short-lived bodies of water such as puddles or temporary pools. In other cases, a species might spend winter in the egg stage, only hatching the following spring when there's food available and larval growth can begin. Female dragonflies of some species even scatter eggs over dry meadows that will eventually become flooded. In that case, the eggs don't hatch into larvae until the moisture comes (see above).

Why do dragonflies lay so many eggs?

There are different strategies in nature to perpetuate genes into the next generations. Either you produce many offspring with the aim that a few will make it to adulthood (think fish), or you produce fewer offspring and nurture them to ensure their survival to adulthood (think primates). Most species have reproductive rates that reflect the capacity of their offspring to survive, with the end result being stable populations over time— barring environmental catastrophe.

Dragonfly reproduction involves many offspring, like fish. Dragonflies are not attentive parents to their offspring, although they do usually make sure to lay their eggs in a suitable place. Laying lots of eggs is an insurance policy that some, at least, might survive to adulthood and manage to mate, lay eggs, and start the cycle once again.

Are the seed-like blobs seen on some damsel- and dragonflies misplaced eggs?

Sometimes damselflies (and less often dragonflies) have small egg-like beads on their bodies that are unrelated to egg-laying. These are parasitic mites. Although damselflies seem to tolerate a certain number of mites, a large enough number of parasitic mites will drain body fluids from the damselfly and lessen its overall fitness.

*Damselfly with several bead-like mites on its body: Desert Firetail (*Telebasis salva*).*

A dragonfly larva has a hinged labium that can shoot out to capture prey.
DICK ERCKEN/SHUTTERSTOCK.COM

What are dragonfly larvae like?

Dragonfly larvae are precursors to the adults, with much the same form except for lacking developed wings. From the smallest larva to the pre-emergent instar, the body form remains largely the same, which is typical of insects that undergo incomplete **metamorphosis** (no pupa). Contrast this with butterflies, which undergo complete metamorphosis. The caterpillar looks nothing like the adult that follows. The reorganization of body form that takes place in the pupa—which is anything but a "resting phase"—is nothing short of miraculous.

Odonate larvae are different from adults in three main ways. First, as the larvae go from early to late instars, the wing buds become more evident. Second, damselfly larvae have three leaf-like external gills at the abdomen tip, which are not present in the adults. As larvae, both damsels and dragons lack the abdominal cerci (claspers) they will have as adults.

Third, the larvae have remarkable mouths (see page 46). The lower mouthpart, the labium, is a two-part hinged structure that can shoot out straight to capture prey. Normally it is parked innocuously beneath the head. When it springs into action, it shoots out to capture a meal. In dragonflies, the labium is flattish and has claw-like lobes at the outer end to grab edible morsels. In damselflies, the labium can even be spoon-shaped.

It is not easy to see these amazing mouthparts in action. I have a preserved larval damselfly specimen, whose labium is extended, which is

A damselfly larva has distinctive, leaf-shaped gills at the abdomen tip.
MP CZ/SHUTTERSTOCK.COM

neat to see. And it's fun to inspect the exuviae of various species to check out the amazing mouths. However, since nothing is as dramatic as seeing the labium in action, I recommend you go online and search "dragonfly nymphs catching food" if you want to see some impressive footage.

How long does a dragonfly stay as a larva?

There's no easy answer to this question. Dragonfly species that lay eggs in puddles and other ephemeral ponds tend to have short life cycles. The eggs hatch quickly, the larvae eat quickly through enough instars to achieve size and maturity to emerge, and the adults fly off before the puddle dries out. The process could take as little as weeks.

Other species may overwinter as larvae, and emergence will happen the following spring, or even a spring years in the future if the habitat is at high elevation or latitude where winters are extreme (see page 58). The bottom line is that dragonflies may remain in the larval stage for several weeks or for more than five years—it all depends.

*Brown Cruiser exuviae (*Didymops transversa*) found high up on a cabin window screen.*

What are exuviae?

To this day when I'm teaching on the trail, I talk about "hatch cases" if and when we see them. These are the empty larval shells, the husks that remain after an insect's emergence. They are often tightly secured by their skeleton claws to whatever plant or rock they crawled up on their way to life in the air.

Technically, I should call them exuviae, a plural noun derived from Latin meaning "sloughed skin of an animal, especially of an insect larva." There seems to be some disagreement about how this word should be used. Some books only use this word in the plural (like pants). Other books are happy to use the singular, exuvia. I guess the zoological jury is still out on this adopted Latin term.

You can distinguish between damselflies and dragonflies by their exuviae, and their shapes fit with the creatures they become. Damselfly exuviae have three paddle-like tails and are skinny and frail-looking; dragonfly exuviae are chunky and have various spines. When scientists survey wetland areas to assess which odonates live there, counting adult odes in the air is difficult. Finding exuviae is another story. By taking a census of exuviae around a pond or along a riverbank, scientists can get a better picture of which species are breeding there and in what numbers and not just count those adults they happen to see fly by.

Some watery habitats are not easy to access. In Bitter Lakes National Wildlife Refuge in New Mexico, the valley has many small sinkhole lakes with steep and fragile edges. As a way of learning which dragonfly and damselfly species inhabited the area, researchers built small wire mesh ladders that the odonates could use for an assisted emergence. Water chemistry varies considerably in mineral content and species can be limited to specific sinkholes. By checking the ladders for the exuviae concentrated there, it was possible to learn which species grew up in which conditions.

How do dragonflies "know" when to emerge?

After a period of time growing through a number of larval instars, the time comes for a dragonfly to emerge as an adult and fly away to meet, mate, and eventually complete its life cycle. In preparation, larvae stop eating a few days beforehand and come towards the shallows in anticipation of the ultimate transformation. The timing of emergence in spring is largely determined by rising water temperatures, influenced, of course, by air temperatures. Day length probably also affects the timing. Some species mass emerge when the conditions are right. This is a strategy with mixed blessings. Many individuals hatching synchronously reduce the risk that any one individual will be snapped up by a predator. On the other hand, a mass of dragonflies emerging might be conspicuous enough to draw in predators from the entire surrounding area. Many species start their emergence during the night, so that their time of greatest vulnerability comes under cover of darkness.

There's another issue in play, too. If weather turns nasty when larvae are about to emerge, they can stall the process for a few days. But if, by unlucky timing, emergence is already underway when the storm hits, then a huge number of teneral odes will fail to make it to adulthood.

What is meant by the rendezvous?

Dragonflies spend time away from the water after they first emerge and until they sexually mature. At that point, they need to get to the right place at the right time to meet up with others of their kind. The name given to the location where dragonflies meet to partner up and mate is called either the encounter site or the **rendezvous**. Generally, the rendezvous is close to the place where eggs will eventually be laid. Sometimes the rendezvous is as simple as flecks of sunshine in a forest clearing back from the water.

Males usually arrive at the rendezvous slightly earlier in the season and slightly earlier in the day than the females. The males hang around there, checking out places with high-quality egg-laying potential, and some of them stake out territories before the females show up. When the females arrive on the scene, the males are already somewhat spaced apart and ready to grab a potential mate. They may copulate then and there or move a short distance away.

Mating doesn't always happen in such an orderly way. It can be much more opportunistic. Males will also grab females on the feeding grounds, or when they are en route to the water if they get a chance. It's a matter of "seize the day" for male dragonflies. Sometimes, pairing will take place at roosting sites. When a pair moves out to get to the water, other males may sometimes be hanging around in case tandem pairs become separated. Then the upstart male will dart in and take his chances.

The rendezvous is not merely a place, but also a time for dragonflies to meet. For many species, there'll be a right and a wrong time of day to show up for the mating scene. A rendezvous is not absolute. The place might shift; a rendezvous may relocate to the shade. Timing may also vary. Young females may turn up earlier in the day than do the older females.

How do dragonfly males and females get together?

When emerged dragonflies have achieved sexual maturity, they must meet to procreate. They meet at the rendezvous, near the water in which the females will later lay eggs (see above). The males turn up first at the right place and right time of day and wait for the females to arrive. How do they recognize females of the right species? First, they rely on visual recognition of color, pattern, overall size, and general behavior patterns—what the birders would call "GISS," short for General Impression of Size and Shape.

When the male sees a likely mate-target, he attempts to grab her by the back of the head (dragonflies) or the neck region (damselflies). If she is receptive, she'll stay in a position in which it is possible for the male to grab her. If she isn't up for a relationship, she may curve her abdomen in a way to repel his advances or to avoid a solid encounter. Assuming both male and female are intent on copulation, the male will transfer sperm from his abdomen tip to the sperm repository underneath his second segment (if he hasn't done so already) and grab the female firmly. She will then curve her abdomen up to meet his segment S2 so she can receive sperm. This can happen in flight or on a perch.

A correct linkage of male and female: Autumn Meadowhawks with female on left.

Does it always go as planned? Mostly it does. Sometimes, however, a male will accidentally clasp another male of the same species, or, less often, a male of a different species. Or a male might grab a female of the wrong species. Fail-safe mechanisms, such as a lock and key fit of sexual organs (see page 23) or a correct fit between a male's claspers and the grabbed female, don't always prevent a mismatch. Occasionally there are cross matings, which may or may not be fertile.

You may also see three-in-a-row connections of various forms. Sometimes the string will be male, male, and female. These mismatches represent a breakdown in the normal reproductive isolation. But there's often a fail-safe mechanism before mating: perhaps the fit is wrong; maybe the two cannot maintain a tandem, or a wheel position; or perhaps the male has the wrong shaped organs to successfully remove sperm from a previous mating. Whatever the final outcome, speed is of the essence in the odonate mating game. If speed comes at the expense of accuracy, maybe that's better than missing the boat.

*Striped Meadowhawks (*Sympetrum pallipes*) take up the mating wheel position.*

What is the mating wheel?

The mating wheel is a heart-shaped linkage between a mating male and female in which the male holds the female by the back of her head with his abdominal appendages while the female reaches under his second segment to acquire sperm that he has previously transferred there.

The mating wheel can take place in the air or on a perch, and often what begins in flight will continue in a secluded place among bushes or other vegetation. Depending on the species, a mating wheel might hold for moments or hours.

Why so long in some species? Males have the tools and technique to remove from the female any sperm remaining from a previous mating. Only then will the current male give sperm to the female. If egg-laying soon follows, chances are he is really the father—guaranteed paternity. Except nature rarely works so simply. Sometimes the female manages to sequester some sperm from both matings, so she also plays the field.

What is "in tandem?"

"In tandem" is the term used when two dragonflies fly (or perch) in a linked position with the male clasping the back of the female's head. The male has special appendages at the end of his abdomen that he uses to grab hold of the female (see page 77). You can find dragonflies in this position either before or after mating.

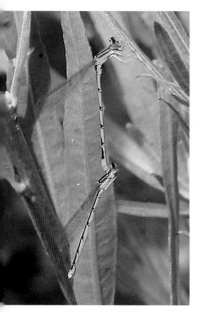

When a male finds a female who appears ready to mate, he must first transfer a bunch of sperm to his secondary sexual organs, which lie on the undersurface of his second and third abdominal segments. He may do this when the pair is in tandem if he hasn't already done so in anticipation of mating. He keeps a firm hold of his female's head, and she then curves her abdomen up to acquire the sperm to fertilize her eggs (see page 77).

After a successful mating, the pair often stays linked in the tandem position until the female is ready to lay eggs. Some species even stay in tandem while the female is laying eggs (see page 64). That way, the male can fend off other males and ensure the eggs laid are fertilized by his sperm.

Double-striped Bluets (Enallagma basidens) *are in tandem.*

Why do dragonflies fly in twos?

When you see two dragonflies flying in close formation like stunt planes, it's a male guarding a female who is getting ready to oviposit or actually laying eggs that he has fertilized. This is termed non-contact guarding. Although he is making sure she successfully lays his offspring-to-be, he may occasionally break off to chase away rival males or even mate with another female. At times, he can be so busy sending off male marauder number one that male marauder number two is able to dart in to grab the female and mate with her.

Why do dragonfly males guard their females?

Dragonfly males may guard females, either by flying close to them and sending off other dragonflies, or by flying in tandem (attached) to them so that it is harder for other males to intrude. In both cases, the reason is that the pair has mated (or is about to do so) and the male is guarding his female from other mating opportunities until after she has laid the eggs that he has fertilized. It's the male's paternity insurance.

What is diapause, and is it a good thing?

Diapause is a phase during which a body's functions are put on hold. The metabolic rate slows down, and growth, development, and metamorphosis cease for a period of time. Diapause can act as a timer to prevent premature development in a season when the animal couldn't survive. For example, larvae might go into diapause to prevent them from emerging late in the season when the adults couldn't make it through the winter. The larvae would then continue with active life the following spring in time to emerge in summer.

Diapause can also act to put individuals in sync with the others of their kind, so that a whole cohort will end up emerging together (see page 74). The ability to go into diapause is a good thing because it enables a dragonfly to synchronize both with the seasons and the activities of other dragonflies of the same species.

Why do dragonflies adopt new wetlands?

Any high-quality wetland habitat is potential dragonfly territory. If existing ponds, rivers, and streams are overcrowded, dragonflies that fail to find satisfactory space within their customary home range will disperse to check out new areas in the vicinity. Their travels may be partly dictated by the direction of prevailing winds at the time. If the dragonflies' established habitat is compromised (dried out, drained, polluted, or short of food), the odes will have to move on. These one-way mass movements in search of food and egg-laying sites can lead to permanent expansion of species' range. They are known as dispersal journeys.

What is the difference between dispersing and migrating?

The differences between dispersal and migration are several. Dispersal generally takes place over a relatively short distance, although it can involve longer journeys depending on wind and weather conditions. Dispersal is forced by changing conditions on the ground, and the journey is one way. By contrast, migration is seasonal and predictable. It takes place on a regular basis and may involve longer journeys. It involves a round-trip, although that doesn't mean the same individuals travel south, then north again, as is the case with migrating birds.

Do many dragonflies migrate?

It's thought that about 16 of the 326 or so species of dragonflies in North America migrate, although details of the migration routes, distances, and returns are only just being discovered. Those dragonflies that migrate may well be similar to the Monarch Butterflies in taking several generations to make the entire round-trip. A joint project called the Migratory Dragonfly Partnership (MDP) has recently been formed. The aim of this organization, according to its website, is to use "research, citizen science, education, and outreach to understand North American dragonfly migration and to promote conservation." Check out their website for ongoing developments (see page 100).

One of the most spectacular feats of long-distance travel involves the Wandering Glider, also known in parts of the world as the Globe Skimmer. Swarms of these dragonflies, together with a sprinkling of other dragonfly species, leave India flying high with the help of a weather event called the Intertropical Convergence Zone. The swarms head south over the ocean to the Maldives and then on to the Seychelles and eventually the African mainland, again wind-assisted and eating windborne bugs on the way. It is an epic journey fraught with perils, including predatory birds that take the same route at the same time.

It's possible to see swarms of dragonflies leaving one place and later to see swarms of dragonflies arriving at another place. But this tells very little about the monumental journey in between. How is that measured? Several years ago, researchers were able to fit some Common Green Darners with miniaturized radio transmitters and follow them for 12 days of their southward migration. Researchers monitored the dragonflies' progress using receiver-equipped Cessna airplanes and ground teams. It turns out the dragonflies flew during the daytime when winds didn't exceed 10 miles per hour and during cooler nights. In between they took time off to refuel.

As technology continues to advance, as tagging appliances become smaller and lighter, and especially as tracking migratory movements by satellite becomes a possibility, there's no end to what scientists might be able to learn.

A roosting Wandering Glider takes a break from foraging or migrating.

Why would a dragonfly migrate when it could survive in place?

It is awe-inspiring to contemplate long-distance insect migrations. Whether it's the Wandering Glider or the better-known Monarch Butterfly, why would such small, apparently fragile creatures, opt to go the distance? The hazards are many: the navigational challenges, the risk of extreme weather, the difficulty of finding food, and the ever-present threat of predation. Alternatively, if the dragonflies didn't migrate, they could (and do) survive winters at high latitudes in the larval stage, tucked securely beneath the ice in a dormant state.

Interestingly, some species, notably the Common Green Darner, have separate populations that either migrate or stay put. It's not yet understood what, if anything, connects the two populations. So why might the separate populations act differently? By migrating, the Common Green Darners (if they are lucky) reach a place of ample food and a wetland habitat where they can winter, lay eggs, and start the life cycle once again. After the larvae hatch, they grow into adults that make their way north to new territory. They arrive in the higher latitudes early in the season, when the local larvae are still deep beneath the ice and far from emergence. The newcomers have an advantage because they arrived earlier in the season. Additionally, having two reproductive locations may be reproductive bet-hedging. Meanwhile, though the life cycle might be slowed down for the stationary subset of Common Green Darners, possibly taking extra years in the larval stage, at least they avoid the hazards of global travel.

At what altitude do dragonflies migrate?

This is not an easy number to come by, as dragonfly migration studies are in the early days. However, a BBC report on the amazing migration of Wandering Gliders from India to Africa claims that these dragonflies fly at up to 6,300 meters (more than 20,000 feet)—higher than any other migrating odonate so far studied.

How far can dragonflies fly?

Migrating dragonflies can fly from India to South Africa, roughly 7,000 kilometers (over 4,340 miles), with the wind behind them. That's a long way for a little insect! Recent work suggests that the dragonflies probably begin this migration in Northern India or possibly even farther northeast, which would make the journey even longer than scientists first thought. Most of a dragonfly's daily flying will be on a much more modest scale, and damselflies probably spend their entire adult lives flying only a matter of meters around their home ponds or riverbanks.

How can scientists discover migration details?

One of the most recent tracking projects followed Common Green Darners by fastening minute radio transmitters to their bodies with superglue and eyelash adhesive. Scientists tracked the insects for about a week until the batteries gave out. Researchers hope that soon it will be possible and affordable to track migrations by satellite.

Weather radar can pick up large insect swarms. Knowing this, some entomologists started using radar tracking as a tool to learn more about the migration and dispersal of insects. Now the practice is fairly widespread, but the swarms most likely to be tracked are pest species. That way, agricultural interests can get an early heads-up on potential crop damage. So far, tracking dragonfly swarms is in its early days.

Dragonflies and Us

What do different people around the world think of dragonflies?

Throughout history, people around the world have noticed and tried to explain or rationalize things they saw in nature. Some of the stories seem strange and fanciful in light of contemporary scientific knowledge, but they were widely accepted in the past. We label these "myths" and may dismiss them, or we can simply enjoy them for the insights they give us into how people perceived animals in the past.

The Europeans didn't seem to care much for dragonflies. You can tell that from the colloquial names given to these creatures: "devil," "stinger," "snake doctor," "darning needle," and "witch" suggest apprehension, if not fear towards the dragonfly. Stories passed from generation to generation that these insects could sting, pierce your eardrums and penetrate your brain, or even stitch up the lips of gossiping women, profane men, and disobedient children. That's quite a load of negative press.

In most of Asia, the reputation of odonates seems to have been more benign. Dragonflies appeared in haiku poems as symbolic of the seasons, especially the red meadowhawks as emblems of fall. Dragonflies were seen as foretellers of rain and sometimes even of death.

From the Native American viewpoint, dragonflies often symbolized spring renewal and rebirth. Representations of dragonflies appeared in Navaho sand paintings and as decorative motifs on pottery, especially in the Southwest, where you can imagine anything symbolic of water and renewal would be welcome in near-desert landscapes.

Bright red pepper-pod . . .
It needs but shiny wings and look . . .
Darting dragon-fly!
           Matsuo Basho
           1644–1694

Dragonfly haiku by Matsuo Basho, 1644-1694: White-faced Meadowhawk as backdrop.

Have things changed in recent years? I'd like to believe that people are more in tune with the importance of all creatures and the roles they play within their respective ecosystems. Perhaps more people are aware that dragonflies consume "pesky" insects and might be good to have around. I'm sure that more people are looking at these fascinating fliers in recent years, but I'm equally sure many, many people never notice them. That makes me sad for what they are missing. I also know that the questions I'm asked as a teacher-on-the-trail suggest that many of the myths, especially negative ones, are still alive and well, even among people interested enough to come to nature programs.

Are there any dragonflies among state insects?

So far, three states have officially chosen dragonflies as their state insects. Alaska's insect is the Four-spotted Skimmer. Students from an elementary school in Aniak, Alaska, got the campaign under way, and in 1995 it was accepted into law. This large dragonfly ranges through northern North America and occurs across northern Europe and Asia from the United Kingdom to Japan. In 1997, the state of Washington selected the Common Green Darner to be its state insect. This is also a wide-ranging

The Vivid Dancer is the state insect of Nevada.

species. It turns up throughout North America and south to Panama as well as in the Caribbean, some Pacific islands, and parts of Asia. Michigan also unofficially claims this species as its state insect.

More recently, Nevada selected a damselfly, the Vivid Dancer (*Argia vivida*) to be its state insect. The process began with a contest for students to nominate and support their candidate. The delicate Vivid Dancer, the candidate suggested by the fourth grade students at John R. Beatty Elementary School in Las Vegas, won the nomination.

Are there dragonfly petroglyphs and pictographs?

Both pictographs (pictures painted on rock) and petroglyphs (images carved or inscribed into rock) of dragonflies have been found, showing that ancient people were aware enough of odonates to record them on rock. But dragonflies don't seem to be very common in rock art.

Many Native American societies used dragonfly motifs in their art. Pots made by the Mimbres culture found in what is now southwestern New Mexico feature stylized dragonfly icons. Other times, the dragonfly was symbolized by no more than two parallel lines crossing a single, fatter line.

Petroglyphs of dragonflies near Bluff, Utah.

Dragonflies swarm all around in the decorative arts.

Do dragonflies still feature in the decorative arts?

As you develop your searching skills in nature, you'll see dragonflies everywhere you go in the outdoors. Beware! You will begin to see dragonflies everywhere else as well. If you are like me, friends who know your interest will start collecting dragonfly artifacts on your behalf until you are inundated by them!

Around my house I have a dragonfly shower curtain, dragonfly lights on the patio, a dragonfly garden stake, dragonfly earrings and pendants, dragonfly scarves, a dragonfly nightlight, dragonfly Christmas tree decorations, dragonfly stickers (my grandkids put them everywhere!), dragonfly wall hooks, dragonfly spoons . . . and that's just a start.

Where can I see dragonflies?

Although you can see dragonflies in many places away from water, the best places to see odes in numbers are wetlands. Apart from the obvious places like ponds, streams, and rivers, sometimes quite unexpected places turn out to offer great dragonfly-hunting. My oding friends and I once spend a fascinating afternoon at the sewage treatment facility in Tucson enjoying an amazing variety of odes. Another time, some friends showed me the delights of a concrete, channelized section of river running through the center of Roswell, New Mexico. We stop on country byways whenever the road or track crosses over any kind of seep or stream. We check out reservoir overflows, stock tanks, and pristine backcountry lakes. In other words, we give anywhere a try, and you should, too!

Do dragonflies harm people?

Dragonflies do not harm people. Despite vernacular names that imply biting or stinging, the most harm a dragonfly can inflict on a human is probably a quick nip if you try to grab it. This applies to large larval dragonflies too. Neither larval nor adult dragonflies have stingers of any kind. I suppose a large dragonfly, flying close, may be alarming if you hear the rattling of its wings. Relax! Dragonflies have excellent vision, making them unlikely to barge into you. The only noteworthy victim on record is a scientist who allowed a darner to oviposit in his arm out of sheer curiosity; no doubt he could have shifted the insect with ease, but some researchers will do anything in the name of science!

Do dragonflies carry diseases that affect humans?

Some dragonflies in the tropics, especially around rice paddies, are hosts to species of parasitic flatworms that can infect humans. The way humans become infected is by eating raw dragonfly larvae. I guess if you must eat them, cook them first!

Do people eat dragonflies?

Some people around the world do eat dragonflies, but this practice is not likely to catch on in the United States. We fear insects and reject them as food even though they're abundant, available, and nutritionally rich.

Personally, I'd much rather watch dragonflies than eat them, although I have eaten other insects by choice. During one entomology class I crunched Mopani grubs, chocolate coated ants, and mealworm cookies. All were tasty. Besides, it is estimated that we all eat insect parts all the time. The US Food and Drug Administration accepts up to 80 microscopic insect fragments per 100 grams of chocolate or 60 fragments per 100 grams of peanut butter. We consumers never know for sure what we we're eating.

In Bali, an island that's part of Indonesia, people catch both adult and larval dragonflies for food. Sometimes they grill the dragonflies and sometimes they eat them in a curry containing ginger, shallots, chili pepper, and coconut milk. Yum! One traditional way of capturing enough dragonflies for a meal is to catch them with a long stick primed with a sticky substance that will easily catch the odes. It's kind of like collecting grit on a dropped popsicle!

Are there endangered dragonfly species?

Few people rally to save a dragonfly species, or, indeed, any insect species—except the all-important pollinators, without whom we'd have no fruit or crops. But there *are* endangered and threatened dragonflies. They just rarely hit the headlines.

As with any animals that rely on wetland environments, dragonflies die off or thrive according to what happens to wetlands. When we plow prairie potholes to grow more crops, when we bulldoze suburban wetlands to make way for housing, when we channel rivers to prevent flooding, the dragonflies take a hit. It's just one more chapter in an old, old story; to save the creatures, we must save the habitat.

In 2010, it was a red-letter day for dragonfly conservation efforts when the federal government set aside an additional 26,000 acres for the Hine's Emerald Dragonfly (*Somatochlora hineana*), more than doubling the species' living space. This is the only endangered dragonfly in the United States. It lives in four states: Illinois, Michigan, Missouri, and Wisconsin.

Around the world, it's the same story. Preserving habitats is the best way to help endangered dragonfly species. According to the International Union for Conservation of Nature (IUCN) Red List of Threatened Species, 15 percent of the Mediterranean dragonfly and damselfly species are in peril, with eighteen species endangered or critically endangered. It is chiefly due to freshwater scarcity, habitat degradation, and climate change.

Hine's Emerald is an endangered species of dragonfly. GREG LASLEY

What are people doing to conserve and protect dragonflies?

The one endangered dragonfly in the United States, the Hine's Emerald, is the target of special conservation efforts, although the species may not be as rare as scientists initially thought. The preferred habitat of the Hine's Emerald seems to be shallow bodies of water over dolomite bedrock, ideally spring fed and gently flowing to ensure good water quality, and surrounded by grass and sedge meadows. Conservation efforts for this dragonfly have centered on maintaining and improving suitable habitats and making sure storm water runoff is adequately filtered by passing through deep-rooted grasses and sedges, so these important odes get the untainted home sites they require.

The other place I regularly watch dragonflies, the United Kingdom, is ahead of the United States in dedicating special reserves for dragonflies. Perhaps this is what happens in a densely populated island nation where citizen scientists avidly monitor populations of practically everything. The approximately forty species of odonates that breed in the United Kingdom are well documented. With such a small number of species to consider, my favorite field guide—*Britain's Dragonflies* by David Small-shire and Andy Swash—has space to include a key to the larvae, too. I am convinced that great field guides like *Britain's Dragonflies* encourage more watching, and that more watching encourages conservation.

Do people collect dragonflies?

Insect collections have always been part of the study of insects, and dragonflies are no exception. Collections enable accurate classification of each species and provide an essential baseline point upon which future knowledge will build. Collections document which insects populated a region and when they were first found. Some scientists and hobby-collectors continue to collect dragonflies. When the specimens are identified, labeled, and stored at a museum or university, they remain a permanent asset for all the students of odonates.

Dragonflies are short-lived insects, and taking a specimen or two will not cause a dent in their populations. Still, it is not something you should do lightly. Unless you are serious about doing it correctly and you've done your research, be content to capture odes by camera. Many people, myself included, prefer to document by photo. It is much more benign than the killing jar although it may lead to more unidentified specimens than you would wish.

Unlike butterflies, which maintain their colors in museum collections, dragonflies easily lose their color and become brittle and dark. Although they are still good study subjects, they lack that essential magic of a live insect flitting across a pond on a blue-sky day in June.

Are there government regulations about collecting dragonflies?

There are no nationwide regulations prohibiting collecting dragonflies. However, collecting is not allowed in National Parks and National Forests and is prohibited in most state, regional, and local parks and wildlife areas, too. You should always check first what rules apply in the area you are exploring and whether you need a permit for scientific collecting.

Can I hold a dragonfly without harming it?

You can catch and release dragonflies without harming them if you do it right. The standard way is to net the dragonfly by a fast swipe from behind and then to close the net with a quick wrist-flick. Hold the net upside down as you reach in (so that the dragonfly can't fly up and away).

Hold a captive dragonfly with its four wings folded together: Lake Darner.

Get hold of the dragonfly by the wings, being careful to fold all four wings together. It works best if you have dry hands free of sweat, lotion, or bug repellant, and if you do not squeeze too hard. Have a look at your captive from all sides, and if you can, take photographs as memory joggers, before letting the dragonfly go again. Never attempt to capture teneral dragonflies. Their developing bodies are still too frail to withstand any handling.

Many cultures have known for a long time that with patience you can catch a dragonfly without a net simply by creeping up behind it very slowly, reaching from behind its head, and capturing it by the wings. If you succeed, you'll never feel the same way about these wondrous creatures again!

How can I attract dragonflies to my garden?

The best way to attract dragonflies to your garden is to create a pond or other water feature. Even small ponds will provide a habitat for dragonflies if they have enough sun and a variety of vegetation. Only certain kinds of dragonflies are likely to adopt a backyard pond. It will depend on the size of the pond, the temperature of the water, the floating vegetation (if any), and the visibility of the pond in its surroundings. You may have to wait patiently for the first odonates to arrive unless you are close to known populations.

My very small garden pond in Colorado, which is about the size of a child's wading pool and a little more than two feet deep in the middle, has floating water lilies, and sedges and irises around the bank, as well as several bushes nearby. There's a good amount of mud above the liner. This pond is home to populations of Blue-eyed Darners, Great Spreadwings, and possibly Shadow Darners (*Aeshna umbrosa*). I occasionally see other species but have not found their larvae or hatch cases yet, so I must conclude they are not breeding, merely passing by.

I also have a pond with a small waterfall in my yard that attracts damselflies, but none of these damselflies, so far, have bred in the pond. We have to keep that pond mud- and debris-free so the circulating pump will not clog, so the environment is too barren to make good wetland habitat. It is literally for the birds.

Some people advocate raising dragonfly larvae to control mosquito populations in garden ponds, water barrels, and other water features. It can't hurt, but it's probably not enough to make a dent in mosquito swarms. There are also mosquito-eating fish to do the job, but trying to use both predators in the same pond is iffy. Chances are that larger fish

A modest garden pond can offer dragonflies a home.

will find the dragonfly larvae a tastier meal than the mosquito wigglers. If you try dragonfly larvae as a natural control in a water barrel, make sure they have a way to crawl out to hatch: rough sides, or an angled stick, or even a piece of burlap over the edge (good for butterflies and bees seeking a drink, too).

How can I take dragonfly photos?

I am a point-and-shoot photographer, so it is beyond my ability to advise anyone on camera equipment or techniques. Over the years of trying to get identifiable photos of dragonflies, I've learned by trial and error.

Start by taking a photo when you first see the dragonfly, just in case. You might spook it into flight when you move closer for that better shot. Be patient! Always move slowly. Approach the dragonfly from behind if you have an option. If your subject cooperates, try for photographs from various angles so you won't overlook the vital angle needed to find out what species you are studying. Sometimes the side shot of the thorax will be the definitive one. Other times you might need to see the face, the shape of wing patches, or even the wing veining. The nice thing about digital photography is that it costs nothing to snap, snap, snap.

For me, the hardest part of dragonfly photography is trying to capture the image against a neutral background. I am usually so eager to get my photo that many of the results are spoiled by busy backdrops—grass stems or tangled greenery—or ruined by strong light contrast.

I don't have twenty-twenty vision anymore, so I rely on autofocus much of the time. This can be a problem. I expect the camera to "know" what I want to focus on, even when it is a small dot blending in with vegetation. I don't want too much, do I?

How can I contribute to dragonfly science?

The Internet has opened up a whole new way of contributing to the discussion about dragonflies. As a citizen scientist, you may want to submit well-documented photographs to the website Odonata Central to increase the information available about where and when species turn up in this country. If you see migrating dragonflies, you can send a report, including date, locations, and species, to the Migratory Dragonfly Partnership. If you see general swarms of dragonflies, you may like to share details of the location and season of the sighting with the time and place with the Dragonfly Woman, a scientist who tracks dragonfly swarms throughout the country. And if you want to learn more about what others are seeing in your home range, check out local Internet chat groups, of which there are many. My favorite group at the moment is Western Odonata on Facebook. For more information on any of these websites, see the Resources section at the end of this book.

Out and About

The best—and most satisfying—way to discover more about dragonflies and the lives they lead is to get out there and watch! I hope this collection of snippets will help make sense of what you see and make you ask more questions as you come across new and puzzling behaviors. Beware! This pastime is addictive.

Glossary

Andromorph. in species with two female color forms, a female with bright, male-like coloring

Arthropod. any segmented, jointed-legged animal

Cerci (singular: cercus). paired appendages at the abdomen tip, in males adapted to clasp females

Chitin. a nitrogenous polysaccharide that makes up the cuticle

Conspecific. of the same species

Contact Guarding. the act of a male dragonfly keeping hold of the female during egg-laying to foil interference by another male

Cuticle. the shell-like outer layer of an insect

Diapause. a state of suspended development to ride out unfavorable environmental conditions

Dimorphic. having two forms of individuals in a single species

Dorsal. the back or upper side of the body (opposite is ventral)

Ectotherm. an animal whose body temperature is primarily maintained by heat from the environment

Epiproct. the single lower abdominal appendage of a male dragonfly (contrast paraprocts—two lower appendages in damselflies)

Exoskeleton. the outer skeleton, or shell, of an arthropod

Exuvia (plural: exuviae). the shed larval shell(s), or hatch cases

Guarding. contact, or close proximity escorting of a female by a male

Hemolymph. plasma-like bug blood

Heteromorph. a female of duller color in a species with two female color forms

Instar. any one of the larval stages between egg and adult

Labium. mouthpart that acts as a lower lip

Larva (plural: larvae). the pre-adult form of an insect (also nymph or naiad)

Mechanoreceptor. a sense organ that responds to pressure, distortion, or touch

Metamorphosis. the process of transformation from larval to adult form

Naiad. see **larva**

Non-contact Guarding. the act of a male staying near his female to prevent interference by another male

Nymph. see **larva**

Ocellus (plural: ocelli). simple eye(s) sensitive to changes in light intensity

Ommatidium (plural: ommatidia). a single visual unit that with many others makes up a compound eye

Ovipositor. appendage used by female for laying eggs

Paraprocts. two paired lower appendages in male damselflies

Pheromone. a chemical attractant used for sexual communication between members of a species

Pruinose. having a white, blue, or gray waxy coating on the body surface

Pseudopupil. visible dark spot in a compound eye that represents a zone of acute vision

Pterostigma. a thickened, often colored cell near an odonate wing tip

Rendezvous. the locale where males and females go to pair up

Spiracle. small opening in the exoskeleton that leads to a breathing tube (trachea)

Tarsus (plural: tarsi). section of an insect's leg farthest from the body

Teneral. a post-molt stage in which an insect's new exoskeleton is not yet hardened

Trachea (plural: tracheae). tubes connecting to the spiracles, or breathing holes

Tracheole. one of the small endings of an insect's trachea

Ventral. the underside of the body, or belly (opposite of dorsal)

Resources

Field Guides

These are the books I began with, and the books I use now, because they cover the areas in which I mainly look for dragonflies. I acquire field guides in the way laundry catches lint and everywhere I go I try to get local or regional guides. There are many, many great ones and more coming all the time. Check out your favorite bookseller for the latest field guides that cover the areas in which you are interested.

Abbott, John C. 2011. *Damselflies of Texas: A Field Guide*. Texas Natural History Guides. University of Texas Press, Austin.

———. 2005. *Dragonflies and Damselflies of Texas and the South-Central United States*. Princeton University Press, Princeton, New Jersey.

Biggs, Kathy. 2004. *Common Dragonflies of the Southwest: A Beginner's Pocket Guide*. Azalea Creek Publishing, Sebastopol, California. (Also available as an e-book under the title *Dragonflies of California and the Greater Southwest*.)

Dubois, Robert. 2005. *Damselflies of the North Woods*. North Woods Naturalist Series. Kollath+Stensaas Publishing, Duluth, Minnesota.

———. 2012. *Dragonflies & Damselflies of the Rocky Mountains*. Kollath+Stensaas Publishing, Duluth, Minnesota.

Kerst, Cary, and Steve Gordon. 2011. *Dragonflies and Damselflies of Oregon: A Field Guide*. Oregon State University Press, Corvallis, Oregon.

Lam, Ed. 2004. *Damselflies of the Northeast*. Biodiversity Books, Forest Hills, New York.

Mead, Kurt. 2003. *Dragonflies of the North Woods*. North Woods Naturalist Series. Kollath+Stensaas Publishing, Duluth, Minnesota.

Nikula, Blair, Jackie Sones, Donald Stokes, and Lillian Stokes. 2002. *Beginner's Guide to Dragonflies*. Little Brown and Company, New York.

Nikula, Blair, Jennifer L. Ryan, and Matthew R. Burne. 2007. *A Field Guide to the Dragonflies and Damselflies of Massachusetts*. Natural Heritage and Endangered Species Fund, Westborough, Massachusetts.

Paulson, Dennis. 2011. *Dragonflies and Damselflies of the East*. Princeton University Press, Princeton, New Jersey.

———. 2009. *Dragonflies and Damselflies of the West*. Princeton University Press, Princeton, New Jersey.

Smallshire, Dave, and Andy Swash. 2010. *Britain's Dragonflies, Edition 2*. WILDGuides Ltd, Old Basing, Hampshire, United Kingdom.

Other Books

Berger, Cynthia. 2004. *Wild Guide: Dragonflies*. Stackpole Books, Mechanicsburg, Pennsylvania.

Corbet, Philip S. 1999. *Dragonflies: Behavior and Ecology of Odonata*. Comstock Publishing Associates (Cornell University Press), Ithaca, New York.

Needham, James G., Minter J. Westfall, and Michael L. May. 2000. *Dragonflies of North America*. Scientific Publishers, Inc., Gainesville, Florida.

Silsby, Jill. 2001. *Dragonflies of the World*. The Natural History Museum in association with CSIRO Publishing, United Kingdom.

Westfall, Minter J., and Michael L. May. 2006. *Damselflies of North America*. Scientific Publishers, Inc., Gainesville, Florida.

Groups

Dragonfly Society of the Americas and Odonata Central

http://www.odonatacentral.org/index.php/PageAction.get/name/DSAHomePage

This site is a good source of all things ode, including checklists for various regions you might wish to explore and photos galore to help identify that "mystery find." The site is also the place to go for up-to-date information on books and to read back issues of their magazine, *Argia*. The current issues are available to subscribers only.

Migratory Dragonfly Partnership
http://www.migratorydragonflypartnership.org/index/welcome
The Migratory Dragonfly Partnership is a collaboration between government, academic, and conservation groups coordinated by the Xerces Society for Invertebrate Conservation. It aims to "better understand and conserve North America's dragonfly migration."

World Dragonfly Association
http://ecoevo.uvigo.es/WDA/dragonfly.htm
This site includes very readable information sheets and useful links to odes groups around the world.

Other Websites

There are many excellent websites—global, national, regional, and local—that give information on dragonfly photos, organizations, conferences, surveys, and publications. You can find scores of them by searching "dragonflies," "damselflies," "odonates," and other such search terms. I'll share only a few favorites, knowing that website addresses can be as ephemeral as mayflies.

International Odonata Research Institute
http://www.iodonata.net/
This site is run by Bill Mauffray of the International Odonata Research Institute. It contains a variety of Odonata resources and "offers a portal to species lists and images from all over the world."

Northwest Dragonflier
http://nwdragonflier.blogspot.com/
This is an excellent blog maintained by Jim Johnson from the Pacific Northwest. It features a little bit of everything about dragonflies and the photography is truly inspiring.

Slater Museum of Natural History
http://www.pugetsound.edu/academics/academic-resources/slater
    -museum/biodiversity-resources/dragonflies/north-american-odonata/
This website, run by the University of Puget Sound in Tacoma, Washington, has a good page on North American Odonata. Here you can find dragonfly photographs and scans and checklists from various geographical locations.

The Dragonfly Woman

http://thedragonflywoman.com/

This blog is insect based and includes some posts about dragonflies. The Dragonfly Woman also collects and collates information about dragonfly swarms.

Western Odonata

www.facebook.com/groups/WesternOdonata

This regional chat group on Facebook is an open group where dragonfly and damselfly enthusiasts can share observations, post photographs, and ask questions. Its focus is on western North America, and it is a lively forum.

Acknowledgments

I wish to thank several people who have been extraordinarily generous with their time and expertise and, above all, patient with a rank beginner: Scott Severs, who got me hooked on this pursuit; Inez and Bill Prather and Dave Leatherman, who welcomed me on many Colorado ode forays (and especially Bill, who read the draft manuscript and offered his expert input); Richard Larson, who introduced me to the New Mexico dragonflies; David Arbour and Berlin Heck, who showed off many new-to-me species in the August heat of Oklahoma; Kathy Biggs, who urged and encouraged me to become more involved in knowing and tracking the odonates of my own state; and many people in the Dragonfly Society of the Americas and the Western Odonata Facebook group, who have graciously helped this newbie to appreciate what this passion is all about. I also offer heartfelt thanks to John Cooper, who researches likely odes locations and actively encourages me in this all-absorbing hobby.